CELTIC MYTHOLOGY

THE GODS, GODDESSES, AND HEROES HANDBOOK

Everything You Need to Know
about the Mythical Characters of
England, Scotland, Ireland, and Wales

SORCHA HEGARTY AND **ARON HEGARTY**
ILLUSTRATED BY ANNA STEAD

ADAMS MEDIA
NEW YORK   AMSTERDAM/ANTWERP   LONDON   TORONTO
SYDNEY/MELBOURNE   NEW DELHI

Adams Media
An Imprint of Simon & Schuster, LLC
100 Technology Center Drive
Stoughton, MA 02072

For more than 100 years, Simon & Schuster has championed authors and the stories they create. By respecting the copyright of an author's intellectual property, you enable Simon & Schuster and the author to continue publishing exceptional books for years to come. We thank you for supporting the author's copyright by purchasing an authorized edition of this book.

No amount of this book may be reproduced or stored in any format, nor may it be uploaded to any website, database, language-learning model, or other repository, retrieval, or artificial intelligence system without express permission. All rights reserved. Inquiries may be directed to Simon & Schuster, 1230 Avenue of the Americas, New York, NY 10020 or permissions@simonandschuster.com.

Copyright © 2025 by Simon & Schuster, LLC.

All rights reserved, including the right to reproduce this book or portions thereof in any form whatsoever. For information, address Adams Media Subsidiary Rights Department, 1230 Avenue of the Americas, New York, NY 10020.

First Adams Media hardcover edition August 2025

ADAMS MEDIA and colophon are registered trademarks of Simon & Schuster, LLC.

Simon & Schuster strongly believes in freedom of expression and stands against censorship in all its forms. For more information, visit BooksBelong.com.

For information about special discounts for bulk purchases, please contact Simon & Schuster Special Sales at 1-866-506-1949 or business@simonandschuster.com.

The Simon & Schuster Speakers Bureau can bring authors to your live event. For more information or to book an event, contact the Simon & Schuster Speakers Bureau at 1-866-248-3049 or visit our website at www.simonspeakers.com.

Interior design by Sylvia McArdle
Interior illustrations by Anna Stead
Interior images © Adobe Stock

Manufactured in the United States of America

1 2025

Library of Congress Cataloging-in-Publication Data has been applied for.

ISBN 978-1-5072-2388-8
ISBN 978-1-5072-2389-5 (ebook)

Many of the designations used by manufacturers and sellers to distinguish their products are claimed as trademarks. Where those designations appear in this book and Simon & Schuster, LLC, was aware of a trademark claim, the designations have been printed with initial capital letters.

Dedication

For my godfather, John, who kept a spot on his bookshelf for the one I swore I'd write. As usual, I was late. —Sorcha

I would like to dedicate this book to my father, Tony, who first taught me how to tell stories, and to my mother, Maria, who taught me how to paint them. —Aron

CONTENTS

Introduction . . . 6

PART 1
What Is Celtic Mythology?   8

PART 2
Gods & Goddesses   29

Danu and Arianrhod 31	Aengus Óg/
Manannán Mac Lir/Llŷr . . . 35	Mabon ap Modron 62
The Cailleach & Ceridwen . . 41	Boann 67
Arawn 45	Dian Cecht. 70
Rhiannon & Macha 49	Balor of the Evil Eye 74
The Morrígan 54	Lugh Lamhfada &
The Daghda 59	Lleu Llaw Gyffes 79

PART 3
Creatures & Monsters   83

The Daoine Sidhe/the Sith	The Bodach 96
& the Tylwyth Teg 84	Ábhartach & the Baobhan
The Brownie & the Púca . . . 88	Sith. 99
Banshees, Bean Nighes	Redcap. 103
& Cyhyraeths 91	The Dullahan 107

Kelpies & Each Uisce 111	Faoladh/Wulvers/ Gwrgi Garwlwyd 127
Selkies/Merrows 115	
Cath Palug. 119	Finnbennach & the Donn Cúailnge 133
Cù-Sìth, Cŵn Annwn, the Black Dog & Wolfhounds. . . 123	Red Dragon/Y Ddraig Goch . . 137

PART 4
Heroes & Villains 142

Pwyll. 143	Medb. 197
Pryderi. 147	Conchobar Mac Nessa 203
Bran & Branwen 151	Fergus Mac Róich. 207
Manawydan. 156	Deirdre 211
Culhwch & Olwen. 161	Fionn Mac Cumhaill 217
King Arthur 165	Liath Luachra & Bodhmall . . 222
Nessa 170	Sadhbh 225
Scathach. 173	Oisín 228
Cúchulainn 178	Diarmuid 232
Deichtre 184	Gráinne 235
Connla. 187	Uirne. 239
Conall Cearnach 191	Caoilte 242

Further Reading . . . 244

Glossary . . . 247

Index . . . 252

INTRODUCTION

Epic heroism…fierce battles…larger-than-life characters who embody all the complicated dichotomies of life: wisdom and folly, fear and bravery, loyalty and revenge. Celtic myths feature stories of transformation and tragedy, of godlike people and mortals defying impossible odds. Emerging from real geographical places and from groups of people with complicated relationships, the mist-shrouded terrain of Celtic myth is truly a landscape like no other.

Celtic Mythology is a journey into stories that whisper through the cracks of history. In this book, you'll discover key characters' names (and how to pronounce them), summaries of who they are (their origin stories), and the most famous adventures they're involved in—plus, you can enjoy dozens of stunning images of these mystical figures.

The mythology of the Celts isn't neatly written in stone or preserved in a singular, definitive text. Part of its charm is that it has been passed *ó ghlúin go glúin* (from generation to generation), co-created over eons. In particular, the magic of these tales lies in their oral retelling. Though they may briefly rest on a page, they come alive when spoken aloud. Centuries of cultural upheaval have added layers of trauma to these tales, which celebrate perseverance and resolve.

To help make sense of this twilit mystery, this book is divided into four parts:

- **Part 1: What Is Celtic Mythology?:** Turns out, it's not actually about leprechauns. Here, you'll learn more about the complex history of the islands where these tales originated, their people, and the cultural traditions that inform the rich tapestry of tales.

- **Part 2: Gods & Goddesses:** These are the powerful figures who created the Otherworld, a realm where they still remain. The world of the real is said to have been shaped by their bodies, their rivers, and their monuments.

- **Part 3: Creatures & Monsters:** The creatures of Celtic mythology slip from the Otherworld into the mortal realm, thriving in the chaos they bring. Vibrant and unpredictable, they are deeply rooted in the local landscape. Blending ancient beliefs with newer faiths, these stories preserve old rites as folk superstitions. They are a reminder that the Otherworld is always close.

- **Part 4: Heroes & Villains:** Only a chosen few—favored by special abilities or linked by magical bloodlines—could move freely between this world and the Otherworld, matching wits with its gods and battling its monsters. The heroes of these tales reveal the paradox of the human condition as they balance on the edges of all things.

Whether you want to brush up on your Celtic trivia (where did the name of the Danube River come from?), better understand a piece of pop culture (such as the powerful goddess Morrígan, who is featured in Marvel Comics), reconnect with an ancestral lineage, or just enjoy these exciting stories, *Celtic Mythology* gives you a front-row seat for the captivating stories of these valiant, remarkable figures.

PART 1

WHAT IS CELTIC MYTHOLOGY?

Before exploring the stories and fascinating characters of Celtic mythology, it's a good idea to understand the culture behind the tales and figures. In this section, you will find a brief overview of the key historical events that influenced these stories. Milestones such as the arrival of Christianity and the effects of colonization profoundly shaped both the evolution and memory of these myths. Alongside this history and a background of the geography of the region, you'll also find a glossary of some key concepts within Celtic society—such as the "fostering" of noble children and the importance of prophecies. Understanding these cultural touchstones will help you immerse yourself in the world of Celtic mythology.

You'll also be introduced to the limited number of primary sources that preserve these ancient tales. Cultural anthropologists in the late nineteenth and early twentieth centuries compiled into books the fragmented manuscript sources and recordings of oral lore that survived through living storytellers. While these compendiums provide modern readers with a solid foundation of Irish and Welsh myths, they are not a complete and definitive source since so much of Celtic mythology is an oral tradition.

Who Were the Celts?

The first and most important thing to remember about the people referred to as the Celts is that they did not refer to themselves as Celts. They thought of themselves as distinctly different peoples. The term "Celt" is a modern construct, a label applied by scholars to various Indo-European tribes, and largely understood as the group of people who landed in Ireland, Scotland, Wales, Galicia (now the northwest corner of Spain), Cornwall (the southwest portion of what's now England), and the Isle of Man (an island between what's now northern England and Northern Ireland). The shared characteristics of these groups have only been understood in hindsight.

The Origin of the Name "Celt"

The word *Keltoi* was used in ancient Greece as a derogatory term for the tribes living north of Greece. But it wasn't until much later that the Welsh scholar Edward Lhuyd used the word "Celt" in his 1707 *Archæologia Britannica*. This study of the Celtic languages and cultures drew connections primarily between the peoples of Ireland, Scotland, and Wales, linking them together conceptually for the first time. By defining a shared linguistic and cultural heritage, Lhuyd's work cemented the idea of a broader Celtic identity, influencing how Celtic mythology is viewed today.

Where and When Did the Celts Live?

The Celts, as defined by modern scholars, are largely agreed to have entered Europe sometime between 6,000 B.C.E. and 600 B.C.E. The major Celtic tribes of mainland Europe, sometimes called the Continental Celtic tribes, included the Gauls of what is now France and the Celtiberians and Gallaeci of the Iberian Peninsula. Then the Britons, Picts, and Gaels came to the Celtic archipelago—another name for the islands encompassing Ireland, Great Britain, and the surrounding islands. These islands became a refuge for the Gaels in particular, where their myths and stories endured amid the growing dominance of Roman and Norse mythologies across Europe.

Keep in mind that these communities still did not see themselves as a single entity, and there was as much rivalry and threat from each other as from outsiders. These conflicts are clear in the mythological narratives, as this book will show.

The Foundations of Celtic Culture

Though the Celts did not see themselves as a singular culture, the connections they shared can be understood in hindsight, and there is a certain amount of overlap that is useful to understand. These terms and concepts help outline the commonalities found within Celtic culture:

- **Fosterage:** Like most mythologies, Celtic myth mostly concerns itself with high-ranking citizens. Noble children were fostered by other high-ranking families. The ties of fosterage were considered to be even more emotionally close than the ties of blood. These relationships were intended as a way of strengthening alliances throughout the scattered communities and clans and were central to child-rearing.

- **Gender:** There have long been hints in the mythology that the Celtic world was not a patriarchy. Women and men are rulers, judges, druids, and warriors in these stories. A warrior whose name has been lost lived one year as a woman and the next year as a man. These tantalizing hints at a different way of life were obscured by the later culture that came to hold sway, and many powerful female characters were villanized, or had their stories truncated or omitted entirely. Recent research has validated that the Celtic archipelago was in fact a matriarchy. Communities lived in "roundhouses" and genetic testing of graveyards has proved that these were arranged around a clan matriarch.

- **Fian**: As part of their training, warriors needed to spend some time in the wilderness, living off the land. Young warriors returning from fosterage would be expected to spend a year or two in what was called a *fian*—a group or a band consisting of other young warriors—where they would hunt and gather together in the summer months and be hosted by kings in the winter. Two or more *fian* groups were known as *fianna*.

- **Kingdoms:** There is said to have been a "king on every hill" in medieval Ireland. Welsh myths tell of the 154 *cantrefs*, or tribes, of Great Britain. Each *cantref* had its own king or woman-king, whose status was dependent on the status of the area they ruled. We use the term "woman-king" because the Irish language puts both men and women in the same role—literally a king and a woman-king, whereas English differentiates king and queen. The woman-kings actually ruled areas; they were not just figureheads expected to provide male heirs. Celtic society was extremely hierarchical, and everyone was expected to know their place.

- **Kings:** Kingship was not directly inherited without contest as in European monarchies. One had to have a claim to the throne, which was linked to birth, but both physicality and practical ability were taken into consideration before a ruler could take a throne. It was important for a king or woman-king to be physically perfect, as the wellness of the ruler was seen to represent the wellness of the land, and therefore the people. Any injury or illness would necessitate a replacement.

- **Law:** The Brehon Law of Ireland is a system of laws and civil codes that dates back to the seventh and eighth centuries. Surviving manuscripts that outline the laws give a strong idea of how a Celtic legal system was structured and how it functioned. There were no police or prisons; instead, laws were enforced through fines. Fines took status into account—the wealthier the offender, the heavier their fine.

- **"Geographical morality":** In many mythologies, the role of the hero is counterbalanced by the role of the villain, but that is not so in Celtic culture. There are few outright villains and few moralistic heroes. Who was considered "good" and "bad" largely depended on the teller, and where they were standing. For example, the people of Donegal in the northern region of Ireland still consider Balor of the Evil Eye to be a hero of theirs because he brought back wealth and prosperity to his own people and ruled them justly. However, people from farther south, across the majority of Ireland, see him as a villain because he was a king of raiders and a scourge to those who he attacked.

- **The learned class:** Bards (storytellers), druids (priests or magicians), and brehons (judges) were accorded high status and believed to have magical powers. The role of storytellers was to entertain but also to speak truth to power. Satire was the bard's great weapon, and a satirized king would not remain in power for long. Druids appear frequently in the mythology as arbiters between the world of humankind and the powers of the Otherworld.

- **The Otherworld (Annwn):** The Celtic people arrived on the Celtic archipelago to see large, strangely placed stones; impressive dolmens (stone monuments); and hills that looked too perfectly round not to be made by humans. They seemed to point to something more mystical, and the Celts' explanation for these remnants of an earlier (now lost) civilization was the Otherworld. This concept suffuses Celtic culture and mythology. The Otherworld is the dwelling place of the gods and goddesses; it is the place where the dead go; it is the home of the creatures that flit in between. Great heroes can traverse the boundaries between worlds and acquire great wisdom. The Otherworld is always immanent, lying just beside the "real."

- **Geis/tynged**: One of the constant reminders of the Otherworld was the existence of a *geis* (as it was called in Ireland, pronounced "gesh") or *tynged* (as it was called in Wales, pronounced "ting-hed"). These were magical prohibitions placed on people, more akin to a prophecy or a taboo than a curse. A *geis* could be placed on a child by a parent, or perhaps uncovered by a druid. The laying and breaking of a *geis* invoked the powers of the Otherworld, and the breaker of a *geis* would be destroyed by the Otherworld.

- **Place:** The stories of Celtic mythology are deeply connected to place. The homes of the gods and goddesses are real, physical places that can still be seen today. The names of ancient goddesses are carried by the waters of the rivers. These stories came from, and belong to, these fast-flowing rivers, the dwindling forests, the ragged cliffs, and the mournful hills of Ireland, Scotland, and Wales. Each tale reflects the spirit of its place, shaped by the land and its people, who accept the mysterious on its own terms.

Understanding the Importance of Oral Storytelling

A fundamental aspect of Celtic culture was the oral tradition, which prioritized storytelling through spoken word rather than written text. A writing system existed, but writing was considered the first step to forgetting. People believed that these stories truly resided only in the mind, heart, and imagination. This poetic and beautiful idea is true in a wonderful way—but also proved to be a fatal flaw. Countless tales have been lost to religious conversion, conquest, war, and the march of time as the minds they lived in did not survive to pass them on. The stories that exist today are those that were written down.

Keep in mind that there is no "pure source" of Celtic myth. The earliest written versions of many of these tales were made by Christian monks. While their efforts preserved many tales, they also altered them to fit their religious narratives. For example, female figures were marginalized or omitted entirely. No details of pagan worship were recorded, as anything like that would have been sacrilegious!

Beyond those details, we can never fully know how faithful they were to the originals. It remains a topic of scholarly debate, creating unanswerable questions that extend beyond the scope of this book. What they have left is a relatively well-preserved tradition in Ireland and Wales, though sadly the older myths did not survive at all in Scotland.

THE MISSING CREATION MYTH

Given the lack of written history, it is not at all surprising that no Celtic creation myth (typically a traditional story that explains the origin of the world/universe) survives. Several Celtic scholars and writers have attempted to reconstruct a Celtic creation myth, though most of these efforts owe more to imagination than to scholarship. For example, common tropes include the Tuatha Dé Danann, the gods of Celtic mythology, calling Ireland up from the waves. But the older stories tell us that the Tuatha Dé Danann were the fourth or fifth group to settle on Ireland.

THE CELTIC CALENDAR

The Celtic calendar's cyclical nature emphasizes renewal, continuity, and connection between human life and the natural world. It divides the year into two halves—light (summer/autumn) and dark (winter/spring). The threshold of each season was celebrated through four major festivals: Samhain (at the start of November), which marks the beginning of the dark half of the year, honoring ancestors and celebrating the abundance of the harvest; Imbolc (at the start of February), which welcomes early spring and is associated with Brigid, saint and goddess; Bealtaine (at the start of May), which celebrates the beginning of the light half of the year, focusing on protection against scarcity, as the last stores of autumn dwindle and new growth has not yet begun; and Lughnasadh (at the start of August), a harvest festival honoring Lugh, god of skill and craft. Both Samhain and Bealtaine are strongly associated with the magic of the Otherworld. The "veil" between worlds is said to be at its thinnest during these times.

IRISH PRIMARY SOURCES

Let's start in Ireland. Some of the oldest sources were found here, dating back to the eleventh century B.C.E. Though there isn't a single source that captures all of Irish myth, there are a few manuscripts that have been translated and organized into the myths we now know today.

ANCIENT MANUSCRIPTS

These old manuscripts often contained religious passages, mythical stories, and poems. Some of the most important ones are:

- **Lebor Gabála Érenn (The Book of Invasions)**: *The Book of Invasions* is a mythological history of Ireland dating from the eleventh century. It describes the waves of inhabitants that arrived on the island—people who are often linked to Biblical genealogies. The god-like people who arrived in Ireland are presented here, as well as the explanation for their departure from Ireland at the arrival of the Sons of Mil (the Celtic ancestors).

- **Lebor na hUidre (Book of the Dun Cow):** This twelfth-century Irish manuscript contains a mixture of mythology, epic tales, and religious tracts. It includes portions of the *Táin Bó Cúailnge* (*The Cattle Raid of Cooley*), a central epic of the Ulster Cycle, which you'll learn about soon.

- **The Book of Leinster:** This is another twelfth-century manuscript that holds many similar mythological and historical narratives as the others listed here, including the first arrival of Cesair to Ireland and parts of the *Táin* from the Ulster and Mythological Cycles.

- *Dindshenchas* (*Lore of Places*): A collection describing the origins of place names across Ireland through associated myths and legends, *Lore of Places* was compiled between the eleventh and twelfth centuries. It offers insights into the land and its spiritual significance to the Irish as well as beautiful linguistic insights.

MODERN ORGANIZATION OF THE ANCIENT MYTHS

Ancient manuscripts were not compiled with a view to making life easy for modern readers, and so Celtic scholars and translators have organized the Irish myths found in these ancient manuscripts into four "cycles," or stories that are linked together by a common theme or by recurring characters. These four cycles are called the Mythological Cycle, the Ulster Cycle, the Fianna Cycle, and the Kings Cycle.

The Mythological Cycle

Though there is no true creation myth in Celtic mythology, there *is* a concept that the land predates the people. There is disagreement over exactly who settled the land and where they came from, but the most commonly cited people or groups of people are:

Cesair

Cesair is often said to be the first leader of people in Ireland. She arrived from northern Africa in a time that was deliberately invented by Christian monks to tie in with biblical "history." There is some debate as to whether Cesair is a "true" mythological character or a full invention of Christian monks. She is said to have arrived with fifty women of art and skill drawn from all the tribes of the world, and three men. Cesair's people seem to have died out, but every successive invader had to deal with shadowy, seafaring shape-shifters called the Fomorians. A few scholars have made the case that the Fomorians descended from Cesair and her people, though no textual evidence for this survives. One of her followers definitely survived: her husband Fintan, who was able to shape-shift into many animals and birds and lived for over five thousand years.

The Fomorians

Also called the people of the sea, the Fomorians had a tenuous relationship with the land; they mostly lived at sea and had a magical connection to the water. Their origin was never specified, but their main base of operations was on, and underneath, the sea around Tory Island, off the northernmost tip of Ireland. They fought battles against all the peoples who wished to establish themselves in Ireland, and spent a great deal of time raiding the mainlanders.

Partholon

A giant from Greece, Partholon came to Ireland with his people to escape a curse that he brought on himself by killing his own family. His people, the Partholonians, defeated the Fomorians in a magical battle, pushing them back to their island homes and away from the mainland. It was Partholon himself who brought the first cattle, the first guesthouses, and many more firsts to the island of Ireland, including the first murder and the first legal hearing on the land. His curse caught up with him at last, however, and the Partholonians were killed off by a plague.

Nemed

Hailing from Scythia (a region in the ancient Greco-Roman world), Nemed fared the best of the invaders up to that point, settling in Ireland and defeating the Fomorians in battle. He was cruel in victory and forced the Fomorians into hard labor until they rose up against him. He decided to attack them on their island home of Tory and wipe them out. But he underestimated their magical connection to the sea, which they used to scatter Nemed's fleet. Only four ships, with a small group in each, survived: One boat went north and became the Tuatha Dé Danann; one went south and became the Fir Bolg; one went back to Ireland but died out; and one went east to a neighboring island, which was named after Nemed's son Britán Máel, today called Great Britain in his honor, according to Irish myth. (The French maintain they named it after the Britons.)

The Fir Bolg

Survivors of the Nemedian sea battle, the Fir Bolg washed up in Greece, where they were enslaved and forced into hard labor. Their name, which means the "People of the Sacks," came from the heavy burdens they had to carry. They eventually turned their sacks into small round boats called coracles and made a daring escape, fleeing across the sea to Ireland. There, they met in the middle of the island and divided it into its five provinces, making space for all that it is to be human: Ulster in the north for warriors and strife; Leinster in the east for prosperity and hospitality; Connaught in the west for wisdom and mysticism; Munster in the south for poetry and music; and Meath in the middle for kingship and generosity.

The Tuatha Dé Danann

Fleeing the Nemedian battle, these people went north, where they learned magical powers and gathered magical treasures. They returned to Ireland only thirty-seven years after the Fir Bolg. Despite their shared heritage, with both being descended from Nemed, the Tuatha Dé Danann and the Fir Bolg clashed in battle. Three important battles then followed. The first two battles were called Cath Magh Tuireadh, which means "The Battle of the Plain of the Pillars," because poets and bards erected posts all over the battlefield in order to see and record the events.

- **The First Battle of Moytura, or Cét-Cath Magh Tuireadh:** The First Battle of Moytura, near Cong in County Mayo, saw the Fir Bolg (with the help of the sage Fintan) face the invading Tuatha Dé Danann. Although the Fir Bolg outnumbered their opponents, they were ultimately defeated by the Tuatha Dé Danann's superior weapons and magical powers. During the battle, the Fir Bolg managed to take the arm off Nuada, king of the Tuatha Dé Danann. This rendered him unfit to rule. During the battle, the Daghda assumed momentary leadership and allowed the surviving Fir Bolg to settle in Connaught, enabling them to coexist in Ireland.

- **The Second Battle of Moytura, or Cath Dédenach Magh Tuireadh:** After losing their king, Nuada (see the Dian Cecht entry), the Tuatha Dé Danann chose a new king: Bres the Beautiful, who was half Fomorian. They hoped he would be a brilliant king and bring balance and peace between the two peoples, but instead, Bres was a terrible king. He invited the Fomorians in to impose brutally heavy taxes on the Tuatha Dé Danann, humiliated the Tuatha Dé Danann warriors, and (worst of all) was stingy to guests. When he was deposed after a poet's satire mocked him, he went to his father's people, the Fomorians, to ask for help. Each side took seven years to prepare, and in the Second Battle of Moytura, Lugh defeated the Fomorian king, Balor, and claimed the land for the Tuatha Dé Danann. This battle took place in County Sligo, near Lough Arrow.

The Battle of Tailtiu: Through this final chapter in the story of the arrivals of these people, we get the origin for the name of Ireland, and an origin of the Otherworld. The Tuatha Dé Danann lived in Ireland for generations. At last, an old man of a new race arrived and gave high praise to the land around him. The three kings who ruled those lands—Mac Cuill (the King of the Wood), Mac Cecht (the King of the Plow), and Mac Gréine (the King of the Sun)—worried that this praise was coming from a would-be conqueror and put the old man to death. This proved to be a mistake, as the old man's nephew, Mil, was a Celtic warlord.

The Sons of Mil threatened to invade the island, and the Tuatha Dé Danann agreed to face the new arrivals in battle. This is where things get murky. In some versions, the Tuatha Dé Danann retreated into the Otherworld, disappearing from the battlefield. In other versions, this retreat was what created the Otherworld, through the power of Manannán's cloak. And in yet another version, the Tuatha Dé Danann fought a bloody battle and were beaten by the Sons of Mil, the survivors driven over the edge of the cliffs and into the sea.

No matter the variations, thanks to the help of their druid, Amergin, the Sons of Mil prevailed. Amergin named the island after the three goddesses he encountered: Banba, Fódla, and Ériu. The modern, official name for Ireland in the Irish language is Éire, which means "the island of Ériu." "Banba" and "Fódla" were used as code names to talk about Irish independence in the poetry and songs of the colonial period in Ireland.

The Ulster Cycle

The Ulster Cycle is mostly concerned with the Ulaid, a tribe in the north of Ireland, and their conflict with the neighboring kingdom of Connaught. This cycle famously focuses on the great yet tragic hero Cúchulainn.

The Fianna Cycle

The Fianna Cycle is similarly centered around one great warrior—in this case, Fionn Mac Cumhaill. He was the leader of a mighty and independent army called the Fianna, who fought off invaders from across the sea and tangled with Otherworldly forces.

The Kings Cycle

The Kings Cycle is less well known and fell entirely out of fashion in Ireland for many centuries. It deals with the "High Kings" of Ireland, a unifying role that may never have existed in reality. The idea was to have multiple regional kings or woman-kings in turn all obey the one High King of all Ireland, who lived in Tara.

The High Kings who made it into the myths often promoted the concept of the "ideal king" or the paragon of kingship (like Niall of the Nine Hostages and Cormac Mac Airt). These were historical kings whose stories were intertwined with mythological lineages to legitimize their political power. The stories of other High Kings, like Conaire Mór, functioned more as cautionary tales; in his case, the violation of a sacred *geis* brought down utter destruction on an otherwise ideal ruler.

WELSH PRIMARY SOURCES

Similarly to Irish mythology, Welsh myths were scattered through ancient manuscripts and later organized into the *Four Branches of the Mabinogi* (often, this is referred to as the "Mabinogion," a word that is incorrect, since it is a double pluralization of the already plural Welsh word "Mabinogi." For this reason, we use the term "Mabinogi" throughout this book instead). The word "Mabinogi" translates to "moon tales" or "tales of a hero's boyhood."

ANCIENT WELSH MANUSCRIPTS

The most important ancient Welsh manuscripts are:

- **White Book of Rhydderch:** This manuscript dates from the mid-fourteenth century and is the earliest collection of prose in the Welsh language. It contains early Welsh poetry, Christian religious texts translated into Welsh, and some stories of the lives of saints. It is one of the most complete sources of the *Mabinogi*.

- **Red Book of Hergest:** The White Book of Rhydderch and Red Book of Hergest may both be copies of the same older text, now lost. Written a little later than the White Book of Rhydderch, the Red Book of Hergest contains a series of triads, a great deal of poetry, and many stories of the *Mabinogi* that overlap with the stories in the White Book of Rhydderch.

- **The Book of Aneirin:** The sixth-century poem *The Gododdin*, a collection of elegies and one of the oldest surviving Welsh poems, is found in this manuscript, and it contains many stories that offer great insight into the warrior culture at the heart of Welsh mythology.

MODERN ORGANIZATION OF THE ANCIENT MANUSCRIPTS

From these ancient manuscripts, the tales of the *Mabinogi* are organized into four distinct branches (sometimes also called "books"):

- **"The First Branch of the Mabinogi"** focuses on the royal family of the southern Welsh kingdom of Dyfed. Pwyll, prince of Dyfed, encounters the Lord of the Otherworld and does him a favor; then, he meets and eventually marries a woman of the Otherworld, Rhiannon. Their son, Pryderi, is abducted by a mysterious being on the night of his birth, but he eventually finds his way home.

- **"The Second Branch of the Mabinogi"** tells the story of Bran, legendary king of the Isle of the Mighty (aka Great Britain), and his sister Branwen. It outlines Branwen's ultimately failed attempt at forging an alliance between Britain and Ireland through her marriage to the king of Ireland. Pwyll and Pryderi from the "First Branch" play a small role in this story, with both of them taking part in the ensuing war with Ireland, and only Pryderi coming back to Britain (his father, Pwyll, dying in Ireland along with most of the invaders).

- **"The Third Branch of the Mabinogi"** continues the story of Bran and Branwen by focusing on their younger brother, Manawydan, the only one of the three to survive the war in Ireland. Pryderi and Rhiannon come back into this story as significant characters. The kingdom of Dyfed is placed under a curse, but Manawydan manages to break it.

- **"The Fourth Branch of the Mabinogi"** takes the story to another kingdom in Wales, called Gwynedd. This is a twisted tale, with rape and incest driving a great deal of the action. The treacherous Gwydion decides to incite war with Pryderi, the king of Dyfed, in order to gain access to the king's servant so that he and his brother can assault her. His king, Math fab Mathonwy, punishes Gwydion by transforming the brothers into animals for three successive years, commanding them to breed with each other. Gwydion's sister, Arianrhod, is proposed as a new servant to the king but has to magically prove her virginity in order to qualify. Instead, she spontaneously and magically gives birth to two children, one of which turns into a sea creature. The other is raised by her brother Gwydion, who is implied to be the child's father. Pryderi's role in this story is relatively minor, as he dies in the war incited by Gwydion.

Other Welsh heroes include an early version of King Arthur, who went on to become a unifying myth for Great Britain in medieval literature. In these early tales, Arthur rules like any idealized Celtic king, leading an extraordinary company of warriors, including several who appear in later Arthurian myth and many more whose names are all that survive. His great lieutenant, Sir Cai (later Kay) bridges the earlier and later versions of Arthur. A prototypic version of the great Arthurian wizard, Merlin, appears under the name of Myrddin Emrys.

> **NOW YOU KNOW**
>
> Both the Welsh *Mabinogi* and the Irish four cycles are modern arrangements of the old tales. In Ireland, stories were usually grouped by the kind of action rather than the cycle they belonged to (i.e., birth stories, voyages, adventures etc.). Welsh manuscripts arrange tales in "triads" or groups of three, some of which are small fragments and others full tale groupings. Examples of this are the "Three Powerful Swineherds" (see Cath Palug's entry), the three children of Llŷr (Bran, Branwen, and Manawydan), and the Three Exalted Prisoners of Britain (Llŷr, Mabon ap Modron, and Gwair ap Geirioedd), and there are many more examples of things being arranged into threes wherever possible.

THE IMPACT OF CHRISTIANITY ON CELTIC MYTHS

Conversion from what we now call paganism, or the many multiplicities of Celtic beliefs and religious traditions popular in Celtic culture, to Christianity was not a process that happened overnight, but gradually, over centuries. Because Celtic myths were first transcribed by Christian monks, it is impossible to fully untangle the influence of Christianity from these stories. The Welsh stories, which were recorded later, show an even higher reliance on Christian beliefs, as priests filled the role of druids as counselors, the Otherworld became threatening, and the godlike people became belittled and associated with more sinister superstitions, with no custom of reverence for them recorded.

A CHANGE IN EMPHASIS

The effects of conversion can also be seen in the way the stories evolved over time. For example, Celtic folklore continued to speak of the Otherworld, but its character gradually shifted. It became the realm of "little people" rather than the supernatural dwelling place of gods and goddesses. Superstition replaced reverence, and under the new religion of Christianity, other beings with the power of gods were literally downsized, becoming physically smaller and less important. Instead of being honored, they were now to be feared or treated as mere superstitions. The belief in the "other" gods was too strong for Christianity to completely stamp out, so it survived as superstitions about "faeries." They became the thing to blame for a bad harvest or a stolen child and kept a sense of fear about them.

OMISSION OF KEY WOMEN

Heroes who did not fit Christian ideals were simply not recorded. Take the Scottish warrior Scathach, whose name means "The Shadowy One." (The Isle of Skye might take its name from her.) Some scholars believe there was once a whole cycle of stories about her, comparable to the cycles of Ulster or the Fianna in Ireland. But the idea of a warrior woman did not align with Christianity. All that had to be done to erase Scathach's achievements from cultural memory was to *not* write her story down. And her stories, like her name, are now only shadows cast from the male hero she trained, the Irish Cúchulainn.

IMPOSING A CHRISTIAN VALUE SYSTEM

Some characters underwent more subtle editing. Fionn Mac Cumhaill was associated with hundreds of women throughout his mythically long lifespan, but many of these relationships were changed to "marriages" in order to align him more closely with Christian values. Similarly, and more damagingly, Queen Medb, whose legendary sexual appetite was a status symbol in Celtic society, had this characteristic twisted against her by later writers, who considered it evidence of her wickedness.

THE IMPACT OF COLONIALISM ON CELTIC MYTH

British colonialism affected Wales, Scotland, and Ireland. In all three countries, the languages and cultures of the local people were suppressed, often through legal means. In Wales, penal laws were enacted by the British in response to the Glyndŵr Rebellion of 1400, prohibiting the Welsh from obtaining senior public office positions, and directly forbidding the support of "rhymers and minstrels," whose storytelling talents were used to stir up support for the rebellion.

In Ireland, extensive penal laws were enacted in the 1600s to disenfranchise Irish Catholics and prevent them from holding on to or building wealth. Scottish Presbyterians were similarly considered to have a "non-conforming" faith. Though historians disagree on how stringently the penal laws were enforced in either case, there was certainly a massive suppression of education—from 1723–1782, all Catholic education in Ireland was illegal. The languages of Wales, Scotland, and Ireland were also suppressed, and the stories associated with these cultures began to be associated with ignorance, poverty, and illiteracy.

For those seeking to further careers in literary circles, English was the only language to write in. And authors and scholars who were heavily interested in mythology favored Greek and Norse myths over those homegrown. These stories were rich with exotic names and wise lessons, and were often regarded as more "sophisticated" than what remained of the local stories.

A Revival of Celtic Mythology

Despite numerous obstacles, there was a Gaelic revival toward the turn of the twentieth century, as notable authors delved deeply into the wealth of Celtic mythology. The works of W.B. Yeats, Lady Gregory, Douglas Hyde, and James Stephens helped co-create this revival. They added their own flair to the translations of the older stories. At the same time, figures like political activist and actress Maud Gonne and poet Pádraig Pearse drew on warrior mythology to encourage nationalism.

This revival fanned the flames of Irish independence. The 1916 Easter Rising, an armed rebellion against British rule, helped spur the War of Independence in Ireland (1919–1921). Despite Ireland achieving its independence, a brutal civil war followed (1922–1923). Burdened by its association with nationalism and violence, the mythology was once again shunned by Irish people for a generation and more.

Wales and Scotland experienced their own revivals during this time. In Scotland, a revival of the Scots Gaelic language was pioneered by Hugh MacDiarmid (also known as Christopher Murray Grieve) and later carried on by the likes of George Mackay Brown, who notably celebrated life on the Orkney Islands.

Writers like Hedd Wyn, Kate Roberts, and Edward Thomas honored the natural beauty of Wales in poems, stories, and songs, bringing a resurgence of the Welsh language. The effect this revival had on Welsh is evident, as the language is still widely spoken and not as endangered as Scots Gaelic and the Irish language, which are both spoken only in dwindling rural fringes.

Today, freed from the baggage of the past, people are once more delving into the wealth of inspiration in Celtic mythology. It is a playground for the imaginations of modern audiences to revisit the realms of these shared stories, and co-create new and reimagined ways for these stories to live on.

The characters, gods, and creatures in this book were chosen for their cultural importance and enduring relevance. They have been selected for their prominence in mythology, their influence on Celtic beliefs, and how they still resonate today through literature, art, and popular media. By blending well-known icons with lesser-known figures, this book highlights the depth of Celtic mythology and its timeless connection to modern audiences, showcasing themes and values that remain universally compelling.

PART 2

GODS & GODDESSES

The gods and goddesses of Celtic mythology were more than powerful figures—they were otherworldly beings who could move between realms. Their home was the Otherworld, or Annwn, a land of eternal youth and beauty, referred to as the many-colored plains, where magic was the norm. These deities were not necessarily tied to elemental forces like the sun or the tides, as in some other traditions—they were instead linked to the land and seasonal cycles. For example, Lugh has become associated with summer's end, Brigid with healing and the fertility of spring, and the Cailleach with winter. The practices and original ways of worship surrounding them were lost to time, but these connections remain.

These godlike people had the power of transformation and prophecy, and these abilities come to life in individual tales. In addition, they often acted in surprising ways. They could be as benevolent as they were malevolent. This dual nature, both protective and threatening, reflects the cautious attitudes still held about them today, where motorways have been diverted to keep a "faery tree" from being knocked down.

Through their stories, we are introduced to an ancient worldview where these godlike beings can walk among us at certain times of the year, and where myth and reality are closely intertwined, guiding mortals with wisdom, mystery, and power.

DANU AND ARIANRHOD

PRONUNCIATION: DAN-u; ar-AN-rhod
ALSO KNOWN AS: ANU; ARANRHOD

Both known as mother goddesses in Celtic lore, Danu and Arianrhod have inspired a legacy of creative reverence in their honor. Danu, the namesake and maternal figure of the Irish Tuatha Dé Danann, embodies creation, wisdom, and the flow of life. The great Danube River of mainland Europe still echoes her name, reminding us of this great goddess. Over time, however, Danu's stories have drifted away from us, like the waters of that mighty river, yet her essence survives in the tales of the Tuatha Dé Danann, translated as the "people of the goddess Danu." Arianrhod, whose name means "silver wheel," is similarly cosmic in her creative influence and is strongly associated with the moon and sea; fortunately, her role in Welsh mythology is better documented.

Both figures symbolize the endurance of life-giving forces—Danu through the remembrance of her name and possible rebirth of her customs under a different name; Arianrhod through her lineage of Welsh heroes who go on to have Otherworldly associations. They both reflect the customs of honoring fertility, lineage, and natural order, suggesting shared origins in an early form of Indo-European mythology, where goddesses of creation, sovereignty, and cosmic balance took on localized expressions within Celtic tales and traditions.

While Danu is associated with rivers, Arianrhod is associated with the moon and stars and is believed to be a remnant of an older sky goddess. Arianrhod was asked to be the foot-holder of the great king Math fab Mathonwy (who had a curse on him that demanded he must have a virgin hold his feet while he was sitting, or else he would die). He administered a virginity test by having Arianrhod step over a magic wand. She thought she would pass, but instead found out that she had been violated (the implication being that she was raped by her own brother) when the magic caused her to suddenly and spontaneously give birth to twins.

She later ruled her own lands near Caer Arianrhod, a rock formation that is visible at low tide from the village of Llandwrog in northwest Wales. Older tales of Arianrhod in her full power do not survive. (It is not uncommon in mythologies to only preserve stories of goddesses' disgrace, victimization, and bitterness in order to discredit them and take away from their worship.) Nowadays, she is mostly remembered as one who tried to take her anger and public humiliation about her rape out on her son Lleu. Her brother, Gwydion, who is the child's father in some versions of the story, consistently tricked her, to the benefit of the child.

THE STORY YOU NEED TO KNOW

Unfortunately, no stories of Danu remain. It is perhaps the starkest erasure in Celtic mythology—her name only survives in the rivers of Europe and the name of the tribe of godlike people: the Tuatha Dé Danann.

However, in Ireland, goddess-worship had to change to survive, and that may have led to Danu's stories being told under someone else's name. A saintly woman named Brigid of Kildare was named after the pagan goddess Brigid, who is a minor figure and only known for her role in the Second Battle of Moytura, when she paused from fighting to perform the first keening (traditional Irish lament) on the death of her son.

It is likely the traditions that were transferred to Saint Brigid originally surrounded the most important goddess: Danu.

If that is true, then Danu, like Saint Brigid, was a goddess of smithcraft and forgery. She imbued healing magic into sacred wells, making them places of pilgrimage and restoration, where people could leave offerings of cloth, ribbons, and handkerchiefs in exchange for the healing powers of the waters. She also protected livestock, especially in the early months of the year, when they began to give birth to the first lambs and calves. On top of that, she was a master brewer, creating beer and kindling musical and poetic inspiration. She was a particular protector of the vulnerable, spreading her cloak of protection over victims of domestic abuse and women in childbirth.

The first day of February was sacred to her and is remembered in Ireland as Imbolc or Brigid's Day. In folk tradition, she was believed to visit every household in the country on that night. Straw beds were left out for her to rest on. The solar cross (a cross with all four arms of equal length, as opposed to a Christian cross in which one arm is longer) was woven out of rushes to honor her and protect the household from fire. (Rushes are Irish wildflowers with broad leaves that grow by rivers and lakes. They were used as a floor covering in homes before modern carpets.) Any cloth left out to catch the first dew of the morning was imbued with her healing magic and could be used to cure sore throats.

These disparate traditional beliefs in Ireland may have once belonged to a number of different goddesses, or to Danu alone. Because goddess-worship was so thoroughly and deliberately suppressed, we will never know.

Now You Know

You can still visit the old sites of these goddesses that have links in the physical world. The Paps of Anu, or the "Breasts of Anu/Danu," are mountains in Kerry in the southwest of Ireland. (Who doesn't want to hike the breasts of a giant goddess?) If Caer Arianrhod sounds more appealing, it can be seen at low tide from the village of Llandwrog in northwest Wales. In addition, there is another fort that bears her name just inland.

MANANNÁN MAC LIR/ LLŶR

PRONUNCIATION: **MAN-ON-ON MAC LEER/TH-LEER**
ALSO KNOWN AS: **KING OF THE SEA**

Manannán Mac Lir is the god of the sea in Irish myth. The great rider of the sea travels over the waves in his chariot, or his magical boat that moves as swiftly as a breath between destinations. Manannán is a powerful deity, and of the Celtic gods, he is more likely than most to take an interest in the affairs of mortals, often appearing as a trickster and teacher. Sometimes appearing in a near-cameo style, he turns up in many other tales as an instigator for Otherworldly magic, without playing a pivotal role.

His name likely comes from the old word for the sea in Irish: *lir* (*lear* in modern Irish). In addition, the Isle of Man—an island that lies between Ireland and Great Britain—is named after him.

VARIATIONS

In Wales, the sea god went by the name Llŷr. It is mentioned that Llŷr was held captive by Euroswydd so that Euroswydd could marry Llŷr's wife, Penarddun. Penarddun's children by Llŷr became great heroes (Bran, Branwen, and Manawydan), while one of her sons by Euroswydd became the terrible troublemaker Efnisien (who caused so many problems for Bran and Branwen). Few other mentions of Llŷr himself remain.

THE STORY YOU NEED TO KNOW

Manannán Mac Lir can often be seen riding across the sea as if it were solid ground on his chariot. His horse, Aonbárr, was able to travel as swiftly over land as it could over sea and is likely the same white horse that appears in the story of Oisín, ridden by Manannán's daughter Niamh. In many Irish stories, white "horses" of sea foam are also referred to as Manannán's horses.

Like many of the Tuatha Dé Danann, Manannán had objects of great power. His sword's name, Fragarach, means "The Answerer" as, presumably, a great big sword is an appropriate answer to many questions. In addition, Manannán had a special cloak: If it was shaken between any two people, they would never meet again.

Manannán's boat Sguaba Tuinne, or the Wave Sweeper, could travel over land and water. All one had to do was speak their destination aloud and the Wave Sweeper would bring the passenger there before they could draw another breath. This vessel appears in one of the stories of the Mythological Cycle, the Sons of Tuireann, in which three brothers must gather a great *eric* (death fine) for the killing of Lugh's father by going around the world, gathering all sorts of magical treasures. The story is somewhat akin to the Labors of Heracles in Greek myth.

Manannán was the foster father to other great figures in Irish mythology and served as a mentor and guide to several mortals. In one story, he visited the great High King Cormac Mac Airt in disguise and tricked him into giving away his daughter, son, and wife in turn. When Cormac followed the stranger to get his family back, he was led through a strange, allegorical landscape that seemed to operate on a kind of dream-logic. Manannán welcomed him into his house at the end of the journey and revealed the meaning behind all of the strange sights the king had witnessed. He gave Cormac a magical cup that broke into pieces when a lie was spoken over it, but it reformed once three truths were spoken. The king was allowed to keep the Silver Branch, a symbol of the Otherworld that crops up in many stories; often (but not always) it is associated with Manannán. With the wisdom instilled in him from Manannán Mac Lir, Cormac became one of the legendary High Kings of Ireland.

In another story, Manannán encountered the hero King Bran on his voyage to the Otherworld. Manannán, from his chariot, called out to King Bran in his boat and revealed his Otherworldly perspective. Manannán told Bran that he saw not an ocean but a grassy, flower-strewn plain, and that to his eyes, Bran's boat was out of place. Manannán was on his way to meet with another Irish king at the time, and fulfill a bargain to help him out in a war against vicious Scandinavian man-eating sheep.

In the story The Only Jealousy of Emer, Manannán's wife Fand eloped with Cúchulainn, both deserting their spouses. Once the regretful Fand had seen the consequence of her actions, she pled with Manannán to return to her. Manannán accepted and shook his magical cloak between Cúchulainn and Fand, ensuring the two lovers would never meet again.

Manannán is also credited with the creation of the Crane Bag, which holds all of the treasures of the ocean. The Crane Bag is said to be open at high tide but closed at low tide, keeping those treasures forever *just* out of reach of mortal hands. The creation of the Crane Bag is a tragic story, as Manannán accidentally killed a woman who had been cursed by a jealous rival to take the form of a crane. She was able to transform back into her human self just before she died and tell Manannán her story. He decided to make the Crane Bag out of her skin as a way of honoring her and making up for killing her, and the taboo in Ireland against hunting cranes can be linked back to this story.

In some traditions, Manannán may even have created the Otherworld. In some versions of the Mythological Cycle, it is the act of Manannán shaking his magical cloak between the army of the

Tuatha Dé Danann and the army of the Sons of Mil at the Battle of Tailtiu that caused the split between the ordinary world and the Otherworld and allowed the Tuatha Dé Danann to remain in Ireland, hidden in plain sight.

Now You Know

Manannán is the Celtic god of the ocean—in other words, the Poseidon or Neptune of Irish myth. He is much more invested in mortal lives than most of the rest of the Celtic gods, and he continually interferes with mortals to try and guide them toward wisdom, or at least heroism. Perhaps he was here long before any of the rest of the Tuatha Dé Danann, however, and will be here long after the inhabitants are gone from these shores.

THE CAILLEACH & CERIDWEN

Pronunciation: KYLE-YACH; KER-ID-WEN
Also Known As: CAILLEACH BHEARA, THE HAG, THE BRINGER OF WINTER; CERRIDWEN, KERIDWEN

As expected, the "bringer of death" is gruesome and terrifying in many cultures. The Celtic tales use the Cailleach, often translated as "Hag," to represent this figure. In Welsh myth, Ceridwen is a powerful and beautiful enchantress with powers linked to transformation, poetic inspiration, and rebirth. The Irish Cailleach is a powerful and sinister goddess linked to death, winter, and the transformation of the landscape. Both the Cailleach and Ceridwen are depicted as fearsome wielders of transformational magic whose tales demand respect and understanding.

The Cailleach, nicknamed the "Winter Bringer," knows no death herself but endures all winters and returns every year to take away the living. The word *cailleach* literally means "old woman" in Irish and Scots Gaelic, but the Cailleach as a figure in mythology goes much further and denotes wisdom and death in addition to age. The Cailleach is a remnant of a sovereignty goddess who appears as a hideous crone. Descriptions of her in the mythology get very…vivid: hair like straw; skin mottled and wrinkled; limbs twisted with age; teeth like tumbled, mossy gravestones; pubic hair down to her knees, which shows through holes in her filthy tunic.

Older stories of the Cailleach place less emphasis on her aged appearance, and she can even appear as a beautiful young woman. In Ireland, the Cailleach appears in several stories, sometimes as one who has been transformed against her will (from a beautiful young woman into a hag) and sometimes as an initiator into power, turning from her hag form into a beautiful young woman only after being laid with.

She is said to rule Ireland between Samhain (Halloween) and Imbolc (the first of February), and to be a spirit of great wisdom—and great danger. She is often counted as one of the aspects of the Morrígan (the name given to the triple goddess of battle rage).

Ceridwen was a powerful Welsh sorceress. With her cauldron of power, she might have originally been a goddess, but survives in folklore as a witch with powers of prophecy, inspiration, and transformation. Her appearance varies in the stories—in some, she is youthful and beautiful, and in others, she presents a more hag-like appearance akin to the Cailleach. Perhaps it was up to her how she was perceived.

Variations

In Scotland, the Cailleach is also heavily associated with winter and is seen as the protector of the wilderness and wild creatures.

In the southwest of Ireland, a figure known as the Cailleach Bheara rules the waters around the Beara Peninsula, occasionally snatching a handsome young fisherman to keep her company at night. The neolithic cairns (ancient rock formations on tops of hills) at Loughcrew in Meath were said to have been placed by the Cailleach herself as she stepped from hilltop to hilltop in one giant stride. She is a shaper of landscapes, and "undoubtedly a goddess," according to some scholars. Central to the Cailleach's story is transformation of herself, of the seasons, and of the landscape.

THE STORY YOU NEED TO KNOW

Niall of the Nine Hostages, a semi-historical High King of Ireland, was said to have won his crown by embracing the Cailleach. ("Semi-historical" people are real figures who had stories about them embellished with mythological themes.) Niall's claim to the throne had been disputed by his stepmother, as he was illegitimate and her four sons were not. On a hunt with his half-brothers, the kings' sons wandered into strange territory and were struck with a terrible thirst. Each went looking for water, and each in turn found a well guarded by a ferocious-looking Cailleach, with crooked teeth, bent limbs, and an unwashed stench. She offered them water in exchange for a kiss. Niall's brothers refused in disgust, but Niall went a step further and made love to her. After the deed was done, she was pleased with his performance and transformed into a beautiful woman. She explained that she was the embodiment of sovereignty, ugly to win but beautiful to have. Niall is still remembered as a great king, and founder of the Uí Néill dynasty of Ulster.

In Welsh myth, Ceridwen is a shape-shifter and keeper of the cauldron of wisdom. She had two children, a beautiful daughter and a hideous son. She thought she'd better brew a potion of wisdom for the poor boy, hoping that great wisdom would make up for his ugliness.

The brewing of the potion took a whole year, during which time the cauldron had to be stirred constantly. She had a boy named Gwyon Bach stir the cauldron for her. One day, when the potion was almost complete, three drops spilled on Gwyon's thumb, and he put it in his mouth to cool it off. Much to his surprise, all of the potion's wisdom transferred to him in that moment!

Knowing that Ceridwen would be furious, Gwyon fled and used the cauldron's wisdom to transform and hide, with the furious Ceridwen in hot pursuit. He became a hare, and she became a greyhound to hunt him. He became a fish, and she became an otter. He became a bird, and she became a sparrowhawk, a bird of prey. At last, Gwyon saw a pile of corn in a barn and turned into a grain of corn to hide among it, but Ceridwen turned herself into a hen and ate all of the corn, Gwyon included.

Instead of dying, Gwyon Bach transformed inside her, and Ceridwen became pregnant. She was still determined to kill the child as soon as he was born, but she paused when she saw how beautiful the baby was. She instead put him out to sea in a leather pouch, no longer wanting to kill him but not wanting to have anything to do with him either.

The child was found and fostered and started speaking poetry while he was still an infant. He became the legendary Welsh bard Taliesin, who went on to great renown. The *Book of Taliesin* is an important part of medieval Welsh literature, and the bard's supernatural origin story adds to its allure.

Now You Know

The chase scene between Madam Mim and Merlin in the 1963 film *The Sword in the Stone* pays homage to Ceridwen's pursuit of Gwyon, though it concludes with a slightly different outcome. Other themes common in Celtic mythology are the swallowing of a seed or an insect causing pregnancy, which comes up again in some versions of the stories of Deichtre and Conall Cearnach.

ARAWN

PRONUNCIATION: AR-own
ALSO KNOWN AS: LORD OF ANNWN, GWYN AP NUDD

Arawn is the dark and mysterious Lord of Annwn, the Otherworld. He is a great hunter and shape-shifter. He rides a white horse and hunts every day with a pack of white hounds with red ears. As a king of the Otherworld, he is associated with death and guarding the spirits of the dead.

VARIATIONS

A later character in Welsh mythology, Gwyn ap Nudd, may be another version of Arawn. They are both fierce hunters, lords of the Otherworld, associated with hounds and hunting, and linked to what is referred to in numerous tales as the Wild Hunt. Gwyn ap Nudd appears in the story of Culhwch and Olwen as the only one who can hunt the Otherworldly boar. He is also said to rule the Tylwyth Teg, the faery people of the Otherworld in Welsh folklore.

THE STORY YOU NEED TO KNOW

Arawn is known for being locked in a rivalry with Hafgan (who ruled the other half of the Otherworld), but Arawn could never defeat him. All of their fights went the same way: Arawn's first blow cut through Hafgan's armor and shield, mortally wounding him. Hafgan begged for Arawn to finish him off, and Arawn, taking pity on his foe, killed him. The following day, however, Hafgan was always restored to full health.

This same series of events happened year after year, and Arawn began to suspect that it was the second blow that allowed Hafgan to magically recuperate. But he could not bring himself to let his enemy die in such a slow and suffering way. As a hunter, Arawn was used to bringing a swift death to a wounded animal. So, he continued delivering the second blow.

One day, Arawn came upon the mortal king, Pwyll, when Pwyll interfered with his hunt, chasing his pack of hounds off a white deer. Despite being insulted, Arawn saw an opportunity. Pwyll was a famously skilled warrior who now owed Arawn a favor. He demanded that they switch places, taking on each other's appearance and ruling the other's kingdom for a year. Arawn told Pwyll that he would have to fight Hafgan at some point, and warned him not to strike Hafgan a second time.

While he ruled Dyfed, Arawn was a just and wise ruler, if a little more stern than Pwyll's people were accustomed to. The ruse was never discovered, thanks to Arawn's enchantment. After Pwyll killed Hafgan once and for all, Arawn named Pwyll a friend of the Otherworld. He changed their appearances back to the way they had been, and each returned to his own kingdom.

Many years later, Arawn gave a gift to Pwyll's son, Pryderi. He had a herd of incredible Otherworldly animals, which were unknown in Wales. They were like boars, but they were tame and weren't a great risk to the hunter's life because they had no terrible tusks and fearsome bristles. They had soft skin and tender, delicious meat, and they could be fed on table scraps. These wondrous creatures were called pigs and crop up quite a bit in "The Fourth Branch of the Mabinogi."

Arawn warned Pryderi not to give the pigs away, and the warnings of the Otherworld carried great weight. Pryderi knew that breaking this condition would be tantamount to sealing his doom. He was tricked into what he thought was a trade of the pigs for other animals, only to find that he was given illusory creatures who disappeared into mist the following day. Sure enough, this set off a chain of events that led to Pryderi's death. Perhaps he was guided into the Otherworld by the white hounds with red ears that his father had followed so many years before.

Now You Know

As Christianity spread throughout Wales, Arawn began to take on more and more fearsome characteristics. The Otherworld became a place of danger, and its ruler was linked with devilry and demonic aspects instead of the stern and just figure that comes through in the original stories. A surviving folk saying, "Long is the day and long is the night; and long is the waiting of Arawn," evokes a kind of patient menace. Arawn and his hounds have lately become associated with the idea of the psychopomp, beings who guide souls from this world into the Otherworld. Disney's adaptation of *The Black Cauldron*, the second book in The Chronicles of Prydain series, highlights Arawn's influence over the villains of the series, leaning into the shared ominous connection to the dead.

RHIANNON & MACHA

PRONUNCIATION: RHEE-ANN-on; MA-ka

Both Rhiannon and Macha share an association with horses, which some scholars believe links them to the Continental Pan-European Celtic (the Celts who lived on the mainland of Europe) goddess Epona. They are both capable of supernatural speed and both decide to marry mortal husbands. The mortal men in question have little to do but be thankful for their great fortune and try not to mess it up—though in the stories, they always do to some extent. Rhiannon and her husband Pwyll managed to overcome these obstacles, but Macha's story is much more tragic.

In Irish mythology, Macha married a mortal farmer, who foolishly boasted that his wife could outrun the prized horses of his king, Conchobar Mac Nessa. Conchobar forced Macha to race while she was heavily pregnant, and she won the race but lost her twins. Because they had failed to use their strength to protect her, she cursed the warriors of Ulster to lose their strength whenever they needed it most. In older versions of the story, the warriors felt the pain of childbirth for nine days and nights, though some prudish writers called it a "weakness" or "sickness." (It was this curse that emboldened Queen Medb to invade Ulster to obtain the Brown Bull of Cooley.) Macha is often grouped with the battle crow Badb and the Morrígan as the three parts of the Morrigú (see the Morrígan's entry for more information).

The Story You Need to Know

Rhiannon was engaged to Gwawl ap Clud, an Otherworldly suitor and son of a powerful goddess. She was unenthusiastic about the match, perhaps because Gwawl had absolutely nothing else going for him: no great deeds, no kingdom, no notable claim to fame aside from his name and his pursuit of Rhiannon. She had her eye on a mortal instead: Pwyll, the dashing prince of Dyfed. Pwyll had recently won the friendship of the not-very-friendly Arawn, after all, and Pwyll was a warrior of some renown. Rhiannon decided to approach Pwyll, but she didn't want to appear too eager. She put on her golden gown and simply rode her white horse past the prince and all his retinue. Rudely, Pwyll didn't address her at all, but he tried to catch her!

Rhiannon wouldn't tolerate that kind of presumption, so she stayed just ahead of the mortal lord and all his men. Her magic meant that she didn't need to speed up past a relaxed amble while they galloped furiously in her wake. After three successive days of futile pursuit, Pwyll called out to her and Rhiannon immediately stopped to talk with him. All he ever had to do was ask…politely.

They both knew from the start that they were a good match for each other. Rhiannon disclosed that she already had a fiancé, but as long as Pwyll kept his wits about him, they shouldn't have a problem.

At the wedding feast a year and a day later, a disguised Gwawl tricked Pwyll into offering him "anything within my power" and demanded both the wedding feast and Rhiannon's hand. Rhiannon tripped Gwawl up on a technicality: the feast belonged to her. She made Gwawl wait a year and a day for her hand and, in the meantime, set about helping Pwyll win her back.

She made Pwyll an enchanted bag that could never be filled and instructed him on what to ask for. At Rhiannon's wedding feast to Gwawl, a disguised Pwyll asked for enough food to fill his begging bag.

Gwawl agreed, and was soon dismayed to see all of the feast disappearing. Not being able to feed the assembled company would be a huge disgrace to him. Gwawl climbed into the bag in a last-ditch attempt to save face. Pwyll promptly tied the cord around his neck and beat him into submission.

Pwyll and Rhiannon were happily married for two years, but the lords of Dyfed grew concerned at their lack of an heir. Just as they began to pressure Pwyll to set her aside, Rhiannon announced that she was pregnant. Harmony was restored, at least until the night she gave birth.

Rhiannon fell asleep with her newborn son in her arms and awoke with blood on her lips. Her servants told her that she had flown into a frenzy and eaten her own child. Neither Pwyll nor Rhiannon could quite believe it, but they had no other explanation for the child's disappearance. Rhiannon undertook a penance. Every day, she sat on a stump outside the castle's courtyard. To every stranger who passed, she called out, confessing her crime and offering to carry them across the muddy courtyard to the gate on her back.

After four years, a golden-haired youth came to Dyfed. Rhiannon made her confession to him, but he asked to walk with her instead of her carrying him. He told her how he had been found by his foster father and had grown up quickly—despite appearances, he was only four years old! When Pwyll came out to greet the visitor, the resemblance was undeniable: It was their son. Rhiannon named their son Pryderi, which means "worry" in old Welsh, for the worry and anxiety he had caused them.

Years later, Pwyll died in the disastrous invasion of Ireland (see Bran and Branwen's entry for the full story about this invasion). Rhiannon ruled the kingdom with Pryderi's wife, Cygfa, while their husbands were at war. Pryderi was one of only seven survivors. When he returned to Dyfed, he brought his handsome best friend, Manawydan fab Llŷr.

Rhiannon and Manawydan got along right away—so much so that Pryderi suggested they marry. The four of them lived in harmony for an all-too-short period of time. One day, a terrible curse descended on Dyfed, covering the land in mist and leaving Rhiannon, Pryderi, Manawydan, and Rhiannon's daughter-in-law as the only living beings in Dyfed.

The four lived in exile for years and attempted to make a living by crafting useful objects for sale and using magic to dye them blue. But everywhere they went, they put local craftsmen out of business, so they were successively driven out of every town by crafters jealous of the quartet's skills. After a boar hunt, Pryderi impulsively went into an enchanted tower and did not return. Rhiannon berated Manawydan for not trying to rescue him, but she was caught in the same enchantment when she tried to get her son back.

Manawydan eventually broke the curse, and Rhiannon returned to Dyfed, where she learned that the curse had, in fact, been all about her. Her jilted fiancé, Gwawl, had put his sorcerer friend up to it all these years later. Nobody ever got over Rhiannon.

Now You Know

There is a popular rise in neo-pagan communities in the north of Ireland trying to "break Macha's curse" by building community and sharing stories of forgiveness.

The unfillable bag that Rhiannon gave to Pwyll is one of the many mythological magic items that one might expect to find in a Dungeons & Dragons game today, where it is referred to as a "bag of holding." "Rhiannon" is also the title of a famous song that Stevie Nicks wrote and was later released with Fleetwood Mac's 1975 album *Fleetwood Mac*. Stevie became obsessed with the name Rhiannon from a young age after reading a novel inspired by her. Rhiannon remains a popular name in Wales.

THE MORRÍGAN

PRONUNCIATION: MOR-REE-GUN
ALSO KNOWN AS: BADB, MACHA, ANAND, MORRÍGU, THE BATTLE CROW, THE WASHER AT THE FORD, THE SHADOW QUEEN

Shape-shifter extraordinaire—between beautiful Shadow Queen and Battle Crow, or one of her many faces—the Morrígan's presence in stories always incites violence, vengeance, and destruction. Sometimes referred to as a singular character, and sometimes as a triple goddess comprising Badb, Macha, and Anand (referred to as the Morrígu), the name Morrígan most likely means "Shadow Queen" (though some translate it as "Great Queen"). She is associated with conflict, war, and particularly with battle rage, a mindless fit induced in her chosen warriors. Warriors who enter this trancelike fighting state become frenzied and are unable to distinguish friend from foe, sometimes physically transforming. Like many of the Tuatha Dé Danann, she can shape-shift easily, preferring the forms of a carrion crow flying over the battlefield, a beautiful red-haired woman, and a withered crone.

THE STORY YOU NEED TO KNOW

The Shadow Queen appears as an instigator of violence in many stories, particularly in the Ulster Cycle. She appeared in dreams to both the king of Ulster and the queen of Connaught, taunting and encouraging them to strike out against one another. She rarely took sides in a battle and revelled in destruction and chaos.

Even when her own people, the Tuatha Dé Danann, were at war, she had to be persuaded by the Daghda to help (he convinced her with a night of wild passion, which probably says something about both of them). Flying in her crow form, her role in the battle was to rain fire on her enemies, scorching them as she soared above; to rain blood upon them, terrorizing them; and to emit a piercing screech so none would sleep for three days and three nights before battle commenced. It's no wonder the Daghda wanted her on his side.

The Morrígan paid special attention to certain heroes, though this didn't necessarily make life any easier for them. Notably, she offered her help (and sex) to Cúchulainn, but when rejected by the young hero, she swore vengeance upon him. She did this by confronting him during a battle, first as a wolf (who bit his arm), then as an eel (who tripped him when he was fighting in the river), and finally as a stampeding cow (who tried to trample him). Though he got the better of her each time, she tricked him into healing her wounds and vowed to be the harbinger of his death.

The Morrígan is said to have had several children but seemed to be an indifferent mother. She is one of the two goddesses who may have borne the goddess Brigid, and the Scottish warriors Scathach and Aoife were said to be "daughters of the Morrígan," though whether that is meant to be taken literally or as poetic evidence of their skill in battle is unclear.

However, there was one tragic exception. She doted on her son Mechi, but the child was sickly, so she sought out the great healer Dian Cecht. His prognosis was grim: The child had three hearts, with a serpent growing inside each of them, and when they grew to maturity they would burst out of his chest and destroy the world, killing Mechi in the process. There was no hope for the child at all—moreover, the only hope for the world was to kill the boy before the serpents could hatch.

Surprising nobody, the Morrígan refused to let her child be killed and took Mechi home, declaring that she cared more for her son than for the world and would care for him as long as he lived, even if that meant the destruction of herself and everyone else. Dian Cecht appealed to the three kings of the Tuatha Dé Danann (Mac Cuill, Mac Cecht, and Mac Gréine) for help. The kings waited until the Morrígan was drawn away from her home by a battle, then took their chance to kill Mechi.

Necessary though that task was, the kings chose a particularly brutal method. They hunted the child with their hounds, dismembered him on a hillside, burned his body in a fire, and scattered the ashes in the river. The three deaths (dismemberment, burning, and drowning) may point to an ancient method of sacrifice, as the triple death killed beyond any hope of reincarnation. The serpents needed to be annihilated, and the child was collateral damage.

Some might say that Mechi's murder fueled the Morrígan's fury at the world, or even caused it, but we should remember that she was in love with destruction and battle long before her son was ever born.

Now You Know

The Morrígan is a constant figure in pop culture, appearing in the 2000s–2010s Canadian TV shows *Sanctuary* and *Lost Girl*. She is also featured as a powerful Celtic goddess in comic book series, including Marvel Comics and *The Wicked + The Divine*, and appears in several video games, such as *Darkstalkers* and *Dragon Age*. The character Mor (short for Morrígan) in the popular A Court of Thorns and Roses series, is inspired by the Morrígan from Celtic mythology.

The Daghda

Pronunciation: DAG-da
Also Known As: Eochaid Ollathair, the Daghda Mór, The Good God

Nicknamed "The Good God," the Daghda was so called not because of his morality, but because of his great skill: He was good at everything he tried. He is particularly renowned for his hospitality and joie de vivre. Fat, bearded, and barrel-chested, with a tendency to wear his tunics too short, the Daghda had a welcome for everyone—but he was no slouch when it came to fighting, able to wield his battle club as easily as his magical harp.

The Story You Need to Know

The Daghda held three great treasures of the Tuatha Dé Danann: the Cauldron of Plenty, which could feed as many as were gathered around it; his mighty club, which usually a man of ordinary strength could not lift at all, and which could kill nine men with a blow from one end and restore life with a blow from the other; and his magical harp, called the Four-Angled Music, with which he could play any feeling he wished into his audience's hearts. He was even given the task of playing the tunes to turn the seasons.

Once, before a great battle against the Fomorians (see Part 1), the Daghda decided to go and talk with the enemy in hopes of negotiating peace. When he got there, he found that the Fomorians had no intention of negotiating. In fact, they had dug a pit in the soil and filled it with meat and porridge in a mockery of the hospitality that he held so dear.

The Fomorians offered him the meal, expecting him to turn it down, at which point they could take offense and attack him. Instead, he carved an enormous spoon out of raw timber on the spot and ate up every last bit, even scraping the sides down to make sure that he left nothing behind. On his way back to the Tuatha Dé Danann encampment, he had to drag his distended belly along the ground behind him. This didn't stop him from seducing a Fomorian princess along the way. She was so pleased with his performance in bed that she switched sides in the upcoming battle.

The Daghda was also romantically linked to goddesses, such as the Morrígan, whom he similarly seduced before a battle to win her favor, and Boann, with whom he had a child, Aengus Óg.

At the First Battle of Moytura (where the Tuatha Dé Danann and the Fir Bolg fought over the rule of Ireland), the Daghda took control of the Tuatha Dé Danann after their great king Nuada was wounded. Impressed by the courage and resiliency of the remaining Fir Bolg army, who refused to surrender, the Daghda called a halt to the fighting. He gave the province of Connaught to the losing side rather than destroy them.

Under the disastrous kingship of Bres before the Second Battle of Moytura, the Daghda was forced into hard labor, digging forts and subsisting on so little food that he began to waste away. This terrible treatment of a great warrior was one of the resentments that Bres accumulated before he was deposed.

After the Second Battle of Moytura against the Fomorian army, the Daghda's magical harp was stolen. He set off in pursuit with fellow gods Lugh and Ogma, cornering the thieves in a ruined castle. The three warriors were hopelessly outnumbered by the Fomorian thieves, but the Daghda called his harp, which magically flew into his hands, and subdued the enemy by playing them the songs of sorrow, joy, and sleep in turn. These are still held in high regard in Irish traditional music, called the "three noble strains": *goltraí*, *geantraí*, and *suantraí*.

For a time, the Daghda was made king of the Tuatha Dé Danann. As king, he helped his son Aengus Óg gain the rights to his mother's house at Brú na Bóinne, modern-day Newgrange, by asking to be allowed to occupy it for a day and a night. When the former occupant appealed to the Daghda to evict Aengus when he refused to leave, the Daghda ruled that "all of eternity passes in a day and a night," pointing out that the year has a day/night cycle, and that all of time follows the same pattern, and thus the house had been surrendered for all eternity.

Now You Know

Generous, somewhat of a trickster, and courageous and skilled at everything he tried (especially lovemaking!), the Daghda is a study in opposites. A mediator and a warrior, a trickster and a mentor, a lover and a fighter, a bringer of death and life, he combines symbology of the masculine (the club) and the feminine (the cauldron), making him one of many ancient deities around the world who subvert our expectations that ancient societies believed in a rigid gender binary.

AENGUS ÓG/MABON AP MODRON

PRONUNCIATION: AN-gus OWG; Mab-on ap MOD-ron
ALSO KNOWN AS: Aonghus, Óengus, Macan Óc, Mac Óc, Oíngus

Aengus Óg's infectious, lovable nature may have granted him the title of the Celtic god of love—or it might have been the fact that he was born and conceived in the same day, full of unconditional love. Either way, he is often associated with love. Birds literally appeared wherever he walked, perching on his shoulders and singing sweet songs to him.

He helped some of the great lovers of Irish mythology, such as assisting Diarmuid and Gráinne in their flight from the Fianna, and playing a key role in setting up his foster father with a younger woman. His dwelling place is called Brú na Bóinne, today the neolithic site of Newgrange in County Meath, Ireland, where he was said to gather and watch over the beloved dead.

VARIATIONS

A poetic link can be made between Aengus and Mabon ap Modron, a Welsh god who similarly inspired love. In Welsh mythology, Mabon ap Modron's name means "the divine son of the divine mother." This is similar to one of Aengus Óg's alternate names, "Mac Óc," which means "the young son."

Mabon ap Modron's story is shrouded in mystery. He appears in the story of Culhwch and Olwen as one of the hunters who needs to be found to hunt the terrible boar. Arthur and his court knew nothing about Mabon ap Modron except that he was taken from "between his mother and the wall" when he was three nights old and asleep in her arms next to the wall of the bedroom. Arthur's followers went to the oldest creatures they could find, each of whom made a speech about how incredibly old they were, before stating that there was an older creature yet who might know more. Finally, a salmon was able to lead Arthur's men to the walls of Gloucester, where the salmon had heard the lamenting of the imprisoned Mabon. They freed Mabon, and he was instrumental in killing the enchanted boar.

THE STORY YOU NEED TO KNOW

Aengus was born of an illicit romance and retained a fondness for such love stories throughout his life. His father, the Daghda, and his mother, Boann, spent a day together. Through the Daghda's magic, the sun stayed in the sky for a whole year, and Boann's husband Nuada stayed out hunting, giving them ample time to enjoy each other's company. Aengus was conceived, carried, and born in that long day. That's why he was called Óg (young). He was always nine months younger than he should have been.

His father brought him away to be fostered while his mother went on to become a river. Aengus was raised by Midir and Fuamnach until he was of age, at which point Midir brought him to meet his father, the Daghda, who was now the king of the Tuatha Dé Danann. His birth mother, Boann, while she lived as a goddess, lived in the incredible sidhe (faery mound) called Brú na Bóinne (also called Newgrange, which is still a significant site in Ireland). She wanted it to be passed to her son, but it was still occupied by her second husband, Elcmar, and now that she was a river, she was less able to intervene directly.

The Daghda advised his son to wait until Samhain (aka Halloween), and take advantage of the traditions around that night. Elcmar would have to open the door to him, as no weapons were allowed on the sacred night, and Elcmar would have to give him any gift he asked for, within reason. The trick was to make his request sound reasonable.

Aengus Óg presented himself and asked Elcmar, who was not pleased to see him, if he could stay in the sidhe for a night and a day. The following evening, Elcmar came to claim his home back, but Aengus refused to leave. When Elcmar went to the king for help, the Daghda sided with Aengus Óg and explained to Elcmar that all of time passes in a cycle of light and dark, just like a day and night. The months have a light half (when the moon is full) and a dark half (when it is new); the year has a light half in summer and a dark half in winter. All of time is a day and a night, and so Elcmar had given up his home to Aengus Óg for eternity.

Aengus Óg later helped his foster father Midir when he fell in love with a young woman called Étaín. Midir's wife, Fuamnach, was furious at her husband for trying to put a second wife above her and cursed Étaín, turning her into a fly. This did nothing to dampen the lovers' ardor, so Fuamnach sent a storm to blow the fly away. Aengus Óg sheltered the fly Étaín for a time before she was blown into the mortal world and was born as a mortal. Midir's quest to get her back was ultimately successful, and Aengus Óg beheaded his foster mother Fuamnach in retaliation for her treatment of Étaín.

Aengus was also credited in some versions with giving the Fianna hero Diarmuid his "love spot," and so was instrumental in one of the better-known Irish love stories of Diarmuid and Gráinne. It was also Aengus who kept rescuing the fleeing lovers and helping to keep them safe in their epic chase. After Diarmuid's death, Aengus Óg gathered him up and brought him to rest at Brú na Bóinne, where he would wake him up from time to time to talk.

Aengus Óg eventually fell in love himself. A white-haired woman he had never met came into his bedchamber one night and started to play on a golden harp. He tried to ask her for her name, but then he woke up alone. Every night for a year, she came back, playing her harp, then after a year, she stopped coming. By that time, he was deeply in love with her, though they had never spoken. He took to his bed, refusing to get up, in hopes that if he dreamed enough he would see her again. A year passed, then he was diagnosed with a sickness of the heart.

After searching for another year and pulling in help from everyone Aengus could think of, including Queen Medb of Connaught, the Daghda found the mysterious woman's identity. She was Caer, a powerful sorceress, and she spent every other year in the form of a swan. She had sworn never to marry a man who would take her away from the water.

The Daghda and Aengus Óg watched Caer and her fifty handmaidens walk into a lake and turn into swans. Aengus Óg mustered up all his magic, and rather than try to pit his strength against hers and tame her, he matched her wildness and turned himself into a swan to be with her. They flew to the River Boyne, which had once been his mother, next to his home, and some claim they can catch a glimpse of the paired swans there to this day.

BOANN

PRONUNCIATION: BOW-ann
ALSO KNOWN AS: WHITE COW

Boann's name actually means "White Cow," a form in which she sometimes appears. Like many of the Tuatha Dé Danann, Boann shape-shifts easily and is difficult to pin down. A goddess of prosperity, fertility, and poetic inspiration, she is particularly associated with the River Boyne in Meath, which she created and became. The river flows around Brú na Bóinne, today called Newgrange, one of the most significant megalithic sites in Ireland. Now known as a passage tomb of extraordinary construction, built to align with the sunrise on the winter solstice, Newgrange was believed in folk memory to be Boann's dwelling, which she left to her son, Aengus Óg.

THE STORY YOU NEED TO KNOW

Boann was married to a great king of the Tuatha Dé Danann called Nuada, and either had a second husband called Elcmar or was married to Elcmar instead, depending on the version of the story. (Multiple marriages did happen in Celtic mythology, though mention of them caused some issues for the Christian transcriptionists.)

Nuada lost his arm in the First Battle of Moytura, and so lost his kingship, as no person with any physical defect was allowed to hold a kingship. Boann and Nuada settled into an uneasy life after the battle, when Nuada's arm was replaced by a mechanical wonder of articulated silver.

Nuada also had a duty to watch over the Well of Knowledge, because it was forbidden for anyone but he and his attendants to look upon the waters of the well. The hazelnuts that grew over the well soaked up the waters and fell when ripe to feed a waiting salmon, which is probably the same fish tasted by the young Fionn Mac Cumhaill.

Apparently discontented in her marriage, Boann had a liaison with the Daghda. She told the Daghda she could not stay longer than a day. The Daghda magically extended their time together so that the sun stayed in the sky for a whole year, fooling Nuada into thinking that his wife had been gone for only one day. In that time, the lovers conceived a child and Boann went through the entire pregnancy, giving birth to their son before sunset.

Not long after the birth, however, in an apparent act of rebellion, Boann decided to look upon the forbidden Well of Knowledge. The water rushed up at her, striking her in the eye and blinding her in a flash of inspiration and intention. Boann ran, and suddenly, the floodwaters from the well followed her. Her path traced the protective path of the River Boyne around her home at the Brú and out to the sea. She commingled with the crashing combination of the salt and fresh waters, becoming the river herself.

Now You Know

Boann's story reminds us there is a strong connection between Ireland's waterways and rivers to the divine femininity and intuitive inspiration that are found at these fertile places. The story of the birth of the Shannon (Ireland's largest river) is almost identical to the River Boyne story, save for the change of name. The Boyne Valley in Ireland remains a land steeped in fascinating prehistoric remains. Later practices associated drinking the water of the Boyne with poetic inspiration, and the driving of cattle through the Boyne was an important part of yearly protection rituals.

DIAN CECHT

PRONUNCIATION: DE-an KECKT
ALSO KNOWN AS: CAINTE, CANTA

In times of strife and disease, the most sought-after figure is always a great healer. Dian Cecht was the great healer of the Tuatha Dé Danann. He was able to diagnose and treat all illnesses. During battles, he created healing pools for warriors to bathe in and have their wounds healed almost instantaneously. These healing wells are thematically linked to the healing cauldron of Welsh myth, which can even revive the dead (you'll see that cauldron featured in Bran and Branwen's story). The role of the healer is incredibly important in Celtic mythology, and many great healers are attributed near-mystical abilities, with the ability to diagnose the cause of an illness given special importance. Illnesses were thought to have their origin in the body, the mind, or the heart, which suggests that there was some awareness of mental illness and emotional dysregulation in the Celtic world.

A strong tradition of faith healers persists in parts of the Celtic Archipelago to this day. Faith healers take no payment for their services, and are widely viewed as a community resource, even among those who do not believe in their powers.

THE STORY YOU NEED TO KNOW

Unlike many of the Celtic pantheon, Dian Cecht's family tree is fairly well documented. His father was the Daghda, and he had many famous children, including Cian, the father of Lugh, linking him with two other significant deities.

Dian Cecht was so skilled at his healing craft that he could tell how many people were in a house, and what afflicted them, simply by looking at the smoke from the chimney and the patterns it made across the sky. He was the one to diagnose the Morrígan's son and indirectly save the world from destruction.

When the Tuatha Dé Danann had to go into battle against the Fir Bolg in the First Battle of Moytura, Dian Cecht, his daughter Airmid, and his son Miach created a healing well, filling it with herbs and chanting powerful spells over it. At the end of each day's fighting, they placed wounded warriors into the well and tended to them overnight. In the morning, their wounds were healed and they were able to rejoin the battle. Having healthy warriors was instrumental in wearing down their enemies.

The Tuatha Dé Danann suffered a great loss in this battle when their beloved king Nuada, husband of Boann, had his arm cut off. By Celtic tradition, no king with a physical defect was allowed to rule. Dian Cecht was able to fashion an incredible prosthetic for Nuada: a silver arm that could move and grip as well as any natural arm. However, Nuada of the Silver Arm still could not rule by law, so he was dissatisfied by this cure. The Tuatha Dé Danann elected another king to replace the wise and just Nuada, and unfortunately chose…poorly. They selected the beautiful—but vain and cruel—King Bres.

Bres's kingship was a disaster. He had been chosen in part because his father was a Fomorian king, and the Tuatha Dé Danann believed that Bres would be able to be impartial between the two peoples. Instead, Bres encouraged his Fomorian relatives to place grueling taxes on the Tuatha Dé Danann, taking a third of their corn, cattle, and children. Something had to be done, but Bres had so mistreated the great warriors that they were weak from hard labor and unable to resist. There was no alternative for a new leader.

Dian Cecht's son Miach stepped in. He found Nuada's missing arm, wrestling it away from a giant hawk that had picked it up from the battlefield. He discarded his father's prosthetic and held the severed limb to Nuada's shoulder. Covering both the limb and the joint in powerful healing herbs, he chanted over it for three days and nights "bone to bone, muscle to muscle, sinew to sinew."

At last, the arm grew back into its place, and Nuada was restored to his former health. With his physical defect repaired, Nuada was able to take up the throne once more, and a disgraced Bres was chased away—for a little while, anyway.

But far from being delighted with his son's skill in healing, Dian Cecht was overcome with jealousy. He could not stand to be surpassed, even by his own son. He attacked Miach four times, striking him in the head. The first three times, Miach was able to heal himself, but the fourth time, Dian Cecht struck a fatal blow and killed his son.

Miach's healing powers continued even after his death. Where his sister Airmid buried him, medicinal herbs and plants started to grow out from his body. Each plant grew over the exact part of the body that it could heal. Herbs to cure the heart, the bladder, the liver, and the spleen blossomed out of his grave.

Airmid realized what was happening and started to gather the herbs. Meticulously, she laid them out on her cloak in the exact spots that she'd picked them from so that she knew which plant corresponded to which body part. But Dian Cecht's jealousy took hold again.

He waited for Airmid to finish her work before snatching up her cloak and shaking it, scattering the herbs to the four winds. That's why, even though the cure for every ailment in the world exists among the plants, Airmid's work of linking plant to body part is still ongoing.

Now You Know

The idea that nature contains the cure for everything is not unique to Celtic culture, but it is certainly a strong concept within the lore. The healing pool, well, or cauldron is an idea that comes up over and over in Celtic mythology, suggesting that the Celts believed in the curative powers of bathing. The modern trend of cold-water swimming is increasingly popular on the Celtic Archipelago, where enthusiasts plunge themselves into the freezing waters of the sea for its curative and restorative benefits.

Balor of the Evil Eye

Pronunciation: BA-LOR
Also Known As: Balar, King of the Fomorians

Portrayed either as the ultimate villain to vanquish or the greatest conqueror, Balor of the Evil Eye was the most important king out of the several that ruled the underwater people called the Fomorians. (They lived off the coast of the northernmost tip of Ireland, on and under the seas of Tory Island.) He grew to uphold a fearsome reputation, burned into the minds of anyone who saw the magic of his evil eye.

The Fomorians had a magical connection to the ocean and could call upon it when they needed to. They opposed all of the groups who attempted to settle in Ireland, raiding and warring from their base in the far north. They were at the receiving end of ill treatment as often as they were the instigators, with some settlers unsuccessfully attempting to eradicate them entirely.

The Story You Need to Know

The Fomorians were the people of the sea and of the land under the sea, called the Tír fo Thuinn, or Land Under Wave. Their kingdom was a harsh place, with little light and little comfort. But they were excellent sailors, raiders, and warriors. They could call upon the sea and its inhabitants in their time of need, and they could make their way up from under the waves to the land above to find what they needed for their families. They had seven kings at any one time, working in uneasy harmony.

One of the Fomorian kings decided to increase his power. He gathered a group of powerful druids and asked them to brew a potion of death. This task was going to take them a year of uninterrupted work, and they asked for complete isolation while they brewed the potion. The king had a young son, called Balor, who was sternly instructed not to go near the extremely intriguing hut full of strange lights and chanting, and he managed to resist the temptation for *almost* a whole year.

Just as the druids' work was coming to its crescendo, Balor was overcome with curiosity and peeked in through a crack in the wall. The potion, which was just then coming to a boil, shot steam into Balor's eye, with all the concentrated power of death contained in it.

This knocked the young boy back, but when the druids rushed out to see what had happened, he was surprisingly quite healthy. Rather than killing Balor, the potion of death infused his eye, giving him the power of killing with a wink. The rest of the potion was now inert and useless, since all of its power had escaped into the boy's eye.

Having a magical eye-beam that could kill any challengers proved to be a serious advantage for young Balor, who gained a following and was chosen as king in due time. He married a warrior, Cethlenn or Caitlín of the Crooked Teeth, who was known for literally biting the heads off her foes. For a time, the two of them were happy together, swashbuckling their way across the northern seas and taking what they wanted when they wanted it.

Then, Caitlín had a child. On her birthing bed, Caitlín had a vision of the future that left her with a stark warning for her husband: None could kill Balor except the child of his child.

They could not bring themselves to kill their only daughter, so they decided to lock away the baby (Eithlinn) and have no more children. To make sure she didn't feel confined, they made Eithlinn a tower out of glass so that she could see in all directions. To make sure she was not lonely, they supplied fifty handmaidens to tend to her every need. To make sure she had no children, those handmaidens were instructed to never speak to Eithlinn of a man, and certainly never let a man inside the tower. She was not to know that there was any type of human other than a woman.

With his daughter secured, Balor's confidence grew. After all, that prophecy also meant that there was no one in the world who could kill him. He brought prosperity to his people when he stole a magical cow that never ran dry from a Tuatha Dé Danann lord called Cian, son of Dian Cecht. The only blight on his life was when his daughter somehow produced a son from within her glass tower, but he cast the child over a cliff and put it out of his mind.

As time went on, the power of Balor's eye grew even more deadly, and it needed to be covered by seven veils lest it set the whole world on fire. It took ten men to lift the lid of Balor's eye, and ten more with sharpened sticks to point it in the right direction.

Balor rarely had to fight anymore since his fearsome reputation preceded him. Besides, the Fomorians found that they had a friendly face on the throne of Ireland: Bres. He was half Fomorian and beautiful beyond compare. Bres told the Fomorian kings that the Tuatha Dé Danann were desperate to avoid a fight with the Fomorians and offered to let them tax his people for tribute in exchange for no longer raiding them. This was a good deal to the Fomorians, though seven kings meant seven taxes. But Bres didn't object to anything the Fomorians did, so the Fomorians continued to ask for more.

One day, Bres arrived to Tory Island in person. The Tuatha Dé Danann had gotten sick of his leadership, risen up in rebellion, and driven him out. He wanted help from his father's people to win back the throne. He spoke to each of the seven kings of the Fomorians, and five of them, including his own father, told him no—he'd had his chance to rule and blown it.

Balor agreed to help, though. He knew that he would only have to take some of the coverings off his eye to immolate the Tuatha Dé Danann armies and be the hero once more. Unfortunately for Balor, he was not prepared for the general of the Tuatha Dé Danann army to be his very own long-lost grandson, Lugh, who slew Balor in the battle.

Now You Know

One of the inspirations behind Sauron from The Lord of the Rings, Balor's evil eye makes for a striking image, now also seen in countless video games. Balor is often depicted as a one-eyed giant, though the stories never say that his poisoned eye was his only eye. Balor remains a heroic figure to the storytellers of Donegal, where the Fomorians stand as a symbol of the wildness of Ireland that cannot be colonized or contained. The largest theater in Donegal is called the Balor Theatre.

The Fomorians are depicted as an evil race in the Dungeons & Dragons game and in the fantasy book series The Dresden Files by Jim Butcher. They are usually linked to ideas of chaos and evil. This is partly due to Christian influence, which tended to demonize any pagan entities, and partly due to a Christian mindset, which preferred to see things cleanly split into "good" and "evil" sides. The actual Fomorians in Celtic myth are no more evil than the Tuatha Dé Danann are good, though both tend to be depicted in these rather simplistic ways.

LUGH LAMHFADA & LLEU LLAW GYFFES

PRONUNCIATION: LOO LAWV-FAD-A; THLAY THLOW GUH-FESS
ALSO KNOWN AS: LUGH OF THE LONG ARM; LLEU OF THE SKILLFUL HAND

The Irish god Lugh and the Welsh god Lleu Llaw Gyffes are known as highly skilled long-range fighters. They share a common root in Continental Celtic gods, such as the Gaulish god Lugus. Both are fair-haired youths, skillful, and brilliant in many regards. As such, they often fit the idealized version of the godlike beings, and something to aspire toward—though not always.

There is a common belief that these two figures are connected to the sun, which comes from a mistranslation of Lugh into "light." Despite the translation error, their stories still shine brightly among the wide pantheon of Celtic gods.

THE STORY YOU NEED TO KNOW

In Wales, Lleu was born suddenly when his mother, Arianrhod, failed a virginity test that was required to see if she could become the new footholder for the great king Math fab Mathonwy. She gave birth to one child named Dylan, and a second baby, Lleu, was almost overlooked. He was only a scrap of a thing that dropped on the floor as she fled the chamber. Her brother Gwydion wrapped up the scrap and only later realized that it was a baby. He decided to raise him, later presenting him to his mother.

PART 2: Gods & Goddesses 79

Arianrhod saw Lleu as an embodiment of her disgrace and placed a series of *tynghedau,* powerful magical prohibitions that could never be broken without inviting doom, on him: that he would never be named, except by her; that he would never receive weapons, except from her; and that he would never marry a mortal woman. These *tynghedau* were all foiled, though. Gwydion managed to trick his sister into giving the child a name when she met the two of them in disguise and saw her son hit the tendon of a wren with a stone. When she exclaimed at the fair-haired child's skill, Gwydion used that for the boy's name: Lleu Llaw Gyffes means "the fair-haired one with the skillful hand." Gwydion also tricked her into giving the boy weapons, and her final *tynged*, that he should have no mortal wife, was circumvented when Gwydion and Lleu made a woman, Blodeuwedd, out of the blossoms of flowers.

Unfortunately, Lleu's wife Blodeuwedd was unfaithful and tried to have her lover, Gronw, kill Lleu. She first had to discover how he could be killed, as Lleu could only be killed under very specific circumstances: neither by day nor by night, neither indoors nor outdoors, neither riding nor walking, neither clothed nor naked, and by no weapon lawfully made. She passed this information on to Gronw, who only managed to wound Lleu.

Transforming into an eagle, Lleu flew away and was eventually coaxed down from his high perch by his uncle, who once again interceded on his behalf and nursed him back to health. Lleu returned to face Gronw and Blodeuwedd, and Gronw asked if he could place a large stone between himself and Lleu, since he was fearful of Lleu's skill with a spear. Lleu agreed, but threw the spear through the stone and killed Gronw anyway. He later became the king of Gwynedd.

In Irish myth, Lugh has many similar characteristics but was born under different circumstances. His grandfather, Balor of the Evil Eye (one of the seven kings of the Fomorians) was told that he would be slain by his own grandchild. This was revealed to him by his wife, Caitlín of the Crooked Teeth, as she gave birth to the couple's only daughter, Eithlinn.

Naturally, they confined Eithlinn to a glass tower, where she was attended by fifty handmaidens who were forbidden to tell her of the existence of men. A Tuatha Dé Danann lord named Cian managed to sneak into the tower dressed in drag, aided by the druid Birog of the Mountain. Cian and Eithlinn conceived a child together.

In most stories, Lugh was thrown from a high cliff by his grandfather as soon as Balor heard the child cry. In one story that echoes the Welsh tradition, it was Balor who named the child. After he observed him hitting an apple from a tree, Balor exclaimed that the child had a "long hand" (*lamh fada*), a phrase that referred to his excellent aim.

In any case, Lugh did not grow up with his mother either; instead, he was carried back to Ireland by Birog. Some traditions say that he was one of triplets and his brothers became the first Selkies (seal/human shape-shifters). Manannán Mac Lir fostered the boy. Lugh quickly proved to be a prodigy and was able to understand and retain information incredibly well—he only needed to see a skill demonstrated once for him to master it. Manannán encouraged the child, finding more people of art and skill to teach him and fulfill his boundless curiosity.

War between the Tuatha Dé Danann and the Fomorians was brewing as Lugh came of age, and it was well known that the terrible Balor with his poisoned eye was going to be unstoppable. Because he had cheated death for so long, Balor's poisoned, corrupted eye had become so potent that it would set the world on fire if it were fully unveiled.

The Tuatha Dé Danann were gathering their army at Tara, and Lugh presented himself there. The gatekeeper refused to let him in if he did not have a useful skill. Every skill that Lugh listed was rejected, as the gatekeeper asserted that there was already someone with that skill within. After listing off dozens of skills, a frustrated Lugh told the gatekeeper to ask his master if he had ever met any one person with *all* of those skills.

The king at the time was Nuada of the Silver Arm, and he recognized that Lugh must be the Ildánach, or Master of All the Arts. He placed Lugh at the head of the army but kept him away from the front lines, unarmed and surrounded by bodyguards. When the battle commenced, Lugh indeed showed incredible skill and leadership in understanding and utilizing all of the abilities of the Tuatha Dé Danann. When Balor took to the field, he fulfilled the prophecy by picking up a stone from the ground and knocking the evil eye out of Balor's head and onto the army behind him at a crucial point in the battle. Like Lleu, Lugh ascended the throne after this trial and became king.

Now You Know

The "shining god of light" archetype appears frequently in popular culture, and Lugh's influence can arguably be seen in any modern hero/god stories where a bulky brute of a man brandishes a shining sword or spear.

But that's not how he's most remembered today in Celtic countries. Some scholars suggest Lugh's name is linked to the leprechaun, the iconic figure of Irish folklore that has little basis in historical Irish mythology. The term "leprechaun" may have derived from *Lugh-chromain*, meaning "stooping Lugh," reflecting the diminishment of old gods over time. (Others trace the name to *lúchoirp* or *luchorpáin*, eighth-century water spirits bearing no physical resemblance to modern leprechauns.) Whatever its origins, the leprechaun—a cheerful trickster guarding a pot of gold—became a comforting symbol for a scattered people. The character was likely accentuated by the Irish diaspora. In a mythology steeped in tragedy and danger, this playful figure offered a lighter story to carry into the New World, ensuring its enduring presence in Irish tourist shops.

PART 3

CREATURES & MONSTERS

The creatures of Celtic mythology are a varied, fascinating lot, each revealing different aspects of nature and the supernatural, depending on the specific region in which they are found. The creatures show clearly both the links and the differences within Celtic cultures and traditions.

Tales of these creatures often reflected local beliefs in nature's mysterious power. In some tales, the creatures are helpful; in others, they are purely tricksters. They exist to explain the unknown and the terrifying, to give the darkness a voice so we can listen to it, and to express the darker edges of human nature. These creatures paint pictures of alluring adventure, utter destruction, pitiful folly—and the chaotic nature of being alive.

These creatures suggest a belief in a world where human rules do not apply and nature's forces go untamed, inspiring awe, caution, and reverence. Each story is a reminder of a time when the boundary between human life and the supernatural was thin, and the landscape itself was filled with beings beyond ordinary understanding.

The Daoine Sidhe/ The Sith & The Tylwyth Teg

Pronunciation: DEEN-ah SHEE; SITH; TUL-with TEG
Also Known As: The Good People, The Good Neighbors, The Fair Folk, The Other Crowd, The Gentry, The Fae

The gods and godlike beings of Celtic myth were downgraded in their worship after the arrival of the Christian faith, but belief in them persisted and was carried forward in the lore of the Little People. These were beings of great beauty and power but diminutive in stature. They were said to inhabit the wild places, particularly waterways and ancient burial mounds, that were assumed to be the dwelling places of the lords and ladies of the Otherworld; these were called sidhe mounds in Ireland and Scotland. (In Irish/Scots Gaelic, the word "Daoine Sidhe" means "the people of the sidhe mounds," which is shortened in English to the Sidhe.)

The Daoine Sidhe, the Sith, and the Tylwyth Teg—also known as the Good Neighbors—could be kind or dangerous and were spoken of in euphemistically good terms. It was widely believed that they might be listening in on mortal conversations, ready to take offense at any slight. Much of the lore around these Fair Folk revolves around warding them off and keeping them at bay.

THE STORY YOU NEED TO KNOW

The Good People were said to be most active at certain times of the year: particularly Samhain at the start of November, and Bealtaine (or Beltane), which is celebrated on May 1. Ordinary people would avoid going out at these times. Mischievous faeries were known to run amok at Samhain, and Bealtaine was the time of year that the Daoine Sidhe moved from their winter to their summer homes; an encounter with the trooping faeries, the Slua Sidhe, was particularly perilous.

Stories of faery encounters follow a familiar format: An ordinary person accidentally encounters a faery, gets caught up in some faery business, and must decide to play along while keeping an eye out for an opportunity to escape. The courageous person might win great fortune, while the rude or insolent person might be brutally punished. Often, the faeries teach their human companion some simple spell or charm that can, say, turn a reed into a flying horse or allow them to pass through the keyhole of a locked door. Plundering the wine cellars of wealthy nobles was a popular pastime for the faeries and their human companions.

Occasionally, the Good People might decide to steal a person—usually either a male infant or a beautiful girl. Situations that invited the attention of the Good People included accepting compliments, particularly those directed toward an infant; sneezing without receiving a blessing; and walking alone past a place where the faeries were known to dwell. They might steal an infant that was highly praised, leaving behind a log in the shape of the child that would gradually stiffen over the course of several days, leading the parents to believe that their child had died. In Wales, the Tylwyth Teg particularly favored fair-haired children. Charms to prevent their capture included iron, especially from horseshoes and horseshoe nails, or the father's sock hung over the edge of the crib, as the faeries were known to be extremely fastidious and repulsed by foul smells. Young boys were commonly dressed as girls on journeys to trick the faeries, as they preferred baby boys to baby girls.

In a more disturbing tradition, the child stolen by the Good Neighbors might be replaced by a faery changeling, a being from the Otherworld who could not quite fit in. People who feared their child had been swapped would go so far as to engage in child mutilation and even murder. Parents were afraid that a changeling faery was in their home and their real child was still alive with the faeries. Practices to drive out changelings in hopes of bringing back the real child persisted in rural Ireland up until the late 1800s.

On the other hand, some faery encounters left people with great gifts: musical talent from a faery tune stuck in their head; clairvoyance and/or the ability to administer the "cure" (likely for illnesses and rashes); or even chronic illnesses and deformities being removed. Direct monetary gifts might also be given by the Fair Folk, though faery gold needed to be spent quickly as it would turn back into fallen leaves in a matter of days.

People in Ireland, Scotland, and Wales held such firm belief in the faeries that as recently as one generation ago, it was common to build houses without doors facing each other. It was well known that if you had a front door facing the back door of the house, the faeries would use this to move through the house with ease and cause all sorts of mischief. And it is still considered extremely bad luck to interfere with hawthorn trees, as these are faery plants.

Now You Know

The Good People of Celtic folklore likely descended from the worship of pagan gods. These beliefs and traditions were suppressed under Christianity, and most of the surviving lore deals with warding off and avoiding encounters with the "Other Crowd." Movies like *Darby O'Gill and the Little People* (1959) and many of Walt Disney's characters helped cement the image of the fae as "wee folk" living underhill, but the origin of these godlike people was very different. The moral ambiguity of the "Good Neighbors" (i.e., their threatening nature and propensity for stealing children) was wiped away in favor of a much more cuddly persona in popular culture. These days, many people are keen to re-engage with faery lore as a way of reconnecting to nature and earlier belief systems. With the capricious nature of these spirits, what could possibly go wrong?

THE BROWNIE & THE PÚCA

PRONUNCIATION: THE **BROO-NEE** (SCOTLAND); THE **POO-KAH** (IRELAND)
ALSO KNOWN AS: PHOUKA

Whimsical, fickle, and impulsive, the Brownie and the Púca are both benevolent figures of Celtic folklore, their tales woven with both charm and a decent scoop of caution. Brownies share characteristics with similar creatures throughout Europe—such as hobgoblins or house elves. They often appear small in stature and are bound by peculiar rules and customs, offering their assistance in secret (and for no obvious reason) yet vanishing at the first sign of acknowledgment or gratitude.

In Scotland, Brownies are usually depicted as small, shrunken humanoids who come out at night to do household chores. They are either naked or dressed in rags, and they must be given offerings of fresh cream lest they turn malevolent.

The Púca demands respect, though their ways are similarly mysterious. The Irish Púca is something of a catch-all term for a spirit, ghost, or creature that defies easy categorization. They often appeared as a man in a ragged coat, but depending on location, they were also described as a hare, goat, horse, or even a strange barrel! The Púca played more of a trickster role in Irish folklore, taking hapless wanderers on wild rides.

To appreciate these elusive creatures is to glimpse a world where the mundane and magical intertwine. These stories offer both wonder and a warning to tread carefully when dealing with the unknown.

THE STORY YOU NEED TO KNOW

Stories of these generally helpful creatures follow a similar path. Sometimes, the recipient of the good fortune is a feckless, lazy person, and sometimes they are hardworking and put-upon. In either case, it is soon discovered that the chores, domestic tasks, and household duties are being completed overnight, while the household is asleep.

In most stories, the recipient of this good fortune decides to wait up one night to see who is helping them, only to witness a supernatural creature going about their business. If a lazy or ill-natured person is the recipient of this Otherworldly favor, it is sometimes one of their jealous neighbors who will wait up to discover the true nature of their helper.

Often, the grateful person decides to leave some gift of clothing for their supernatural helpers, but this action always results in them leaving forever. Sometimes, the creature is observed donning a new coat or a fresh set of clothes and admiring themselves before declaring that they are clearly of a station above menial tasks, and departing forever. Usually, if they have been helping a virtuous person, there will be no harm done, as such a person has likely saved money wisely over the years. A lazy person, on the other hand, may lose their comfortable job once they have to do the hard work themselves.

The Púca can be a rather more chaotic helper at times. One story tells of a piper who knew only one tune, called "The Black Rogue." He played that well and was too lazy to learn other songs. (Getting to hear a definitive version of "The Black Rogue" is as difficult as finding a definitive version of this story: There are currently dozens of variations available.) But after hearing the piper play, a stranger in a ragged coat asked him to come and play at a birthday party. The piper tried to decline but was swept up onto the back of a horse that now stood in the place of the stranger. He was carried off across the countryside and under the hills to the Queen of the Banshees' birthday celebration. The terrified piper was worried that he would be found out, but a reassuring word from the Púca left him able to pipe all night and come up with better tunes than he had ever heard.

The Púca brought the piper home the following day, but the man found that he once again had no ability to play anything other than his one reliable tune. But the faery music was still lodged in his head, and he spent the following years hard at work to re-create the tunes he had played for the Queen of the Banshees. He never managed to his satisfaction, but the effort led to him becoming one of the greatest pipers in Ireland.

Now You Know

It seems clear that the house elves in Harry Potter's world are directly drawn from the Scottish Brownie, as a gift of clothing sets them free from servitude. Brownies also appear in The Spiderwick Chronicles series by Tony DiTerlizzi and Holly Black, *Dragon Rider* by Cornelia Funke, and Rick Riordan's *Magnus Chase and the Gods of Asgard: Ship of the Dead*.

BANSHEES, BEAN NIGHES & CYHYRAETHS

PRONUNCIATION: BAN-SHE; BAN-NEE; KU-HU-RHYTH
ALSO KNOWN AS: WEEPING WOMAN, WASHERWOMAN

Ethereal and haunting, Banshees, Bean Nighes, and Cyhyraeths weave through the tapestry of Celtic folklore as spectral omens of death. These female apparitions exist on the boundary between the mortal world and the Otherworld, their mournful cries or piercing screams foretelling the inevitable. Unlike malevolent spirits, however, these are not bringers of death—they simply announce it, reminding us of the unyielding certainty that awaits us all.

The Banshee's keening wail echoes through the night, an Otherworldly lament for lives soon to be lost. (See The Story You Need to Know for an explanation of keening.) Many still claim to have heard the cry of the Banshee in Ireland today. The Bean Nighe, bent low in a stream, scrubs blood-soaked garments, each tied to one fated to perish. The Cyhyraeth, though lesser known, shares their mournful duty, its voice a phantom whisper on the wind. These figures are deeply tied to the land and its people, their presence both feared and revered as part of the natural cycle of life and death.

Variations

In Ireland and Scotland, the Banshee (meaning "woman of the sidhe") appears as a weeping woman—sometimes young and lovely, sometimes a withered hag—often combing her hair and keening. She cries for the deaths of certain old Gaelic noble families.

In Scotland, Bean Nighe means "washerwoman." She does not weep but washes the clothing of the soon-to-be deceased in a river. The Bean Nighe washes the clothes of Ewen MacLaine of Lochbuie before his clan's neighborly feud in a tale that claims the origin of the headless horseman (see the Dullahan's entry). This image has deep roots in Celtic mythology, and heroes of the Ulster and Fianna Cycles had their deaths foretold in this way, notably in the death of Cúchulainn and the death of Oisín's fierce son Osgar.

In Wales, the Cyhyraeth has no physical form but is a disembodied voice that cries three times, with decreasing strength, to foreshadow death.

The Story You Need to Know

In all the variations of the tales of these creatures, a cry is heard, foretelling the death of a certain scion of the family. Usually, this person is either in good health or on the cusp of recovery from a long illness, and the portent seems misplaced. However, the object of the foretelling inevitably comes to some tragic end. Their death could come in the form of a sudden accident, an illness that had been thought to be abating coming back tenfold, or some other misfortune invariably carrying them off.

The Banshee rarely has a detailed narrative associated with her, but many families or old accounts place the Banshee's song or cry at the death of a family member. In Ireland and some parts of Scotland, the cry of the Banshee also links to the tradition of keening, or *chaointe*. Keening is the performance of a lament that was held at funerals and wakes. Professional keeners were in high demand at one time, though the practice has all but died out in most places. The Banshee might wail like a keener, or sing sweetly, or simply weep. The Banshee was thought to only cry for those of "pure" descent; that is, families who were descended from the Sons of Mil, who were fully Gaelic and not of Norman or Saxon descent. There are exceptions to this rule, as the Banshee may also appear for, say, a gifted singer of any family.

In the south of Ireland, there is a story of the Queen of the Banshees. She is said to be a Sidhe woman named Clíodhna, who came from the land of promise and was the daughter of Manannán Mac Lir. Disobeying her father's commands, she followed the young Fianna warrior Ciabhán of the Curling Locks to Ireland, only to lose him after a brief love affair. She went to the southwest coast, near Glandore Harbour in Cork, and wailed her heartbreak to the sea. Her father took no pity on her and sent nine waves against her, the last one sweeping her away to drown. In Glandore, her cry is said to still be heard, though only on every ninth wave.

Because of the way myths evolved over time, it is possible that the Banshee is linked with the Morrígan. In myth, the "Washer at the Ford" is also associated with the Morrígan. She appears numerous times, famously foretelling the death of Cúchulainn, the greatest of the warriors of the Red Branch, as he rode to his certain death in his final battle against Queen Medb's armies. This figure is also seen at the end of the Fianna saga, just before the Battle of Gabhra, when the Washer at the Ford washed the armor of the greatest fighter in the Fianna at the time, Osgar of the Many Feats, the beloved son of Oisín. This trope appears in numerous places across Celtic mythology and is usually used for warriors who willingly go to their deaths, accepting their fates and giving their lives knowingly to the cause they fight for.

Now You Know

The Banshee, Bean Nighe, and Cyhyraeth may not wield the power to cause death, but their mournful presence serves as a stark reminder of the inevitability of death. Even the greatest heroes come to terms with this fact, perhaps reminding us to make the most of the time we have.

These figures have also found a place in modern pop culture, blending their mythic roots with contemporary storytelling. Banshees have appeared in the Harry Potter universe, the *Teen Wolf* television show and 2023 movie, and the show *Supernatural*. Marvel Comics also features a character named Banshee. While the 2022 film *The Banshees of Inisherin* (featuring Colin Farrell and Brendan Gleeson) didn't directly reference the mythical creature in the movie, it drew from the cultural resonance of the Banshee as a symbol of inevitable sorrow.

THE BODACH

PRONUNCIATION: BOH-dakh
ALSO KNOWN AS: BODACH GLAS, GRAY CHURL, OLD MAN

The Bodach, who is often paired with the Cailleach or considered her male counterpart, personifies the inevitability of aging and death for men. His malevolent smile hints at these sinister truths. Depicted in tattered, grubby clothing, he chews on a straw with his remaining crooked teeth. A frayed hat is pulled low over his brow, and his hollow dark eyes glint with humor as he watches the approach of death with unsettling amusement.

This mysterious figure of Celtic folklore is both a mischievous trickster and a harbinger of death. Known to haunt rural families during the darkest days of winter, he instilled fear by slipping down chimneys to abduct misbehaving children or signaling the imminent death of a loved one battling illness. His tricks, which often arrived without a treat, carried an ominous edge, further marking him as a forewarning of death. Families believed he could be stopped with salt—a valuable resource in such dire times.

The name "Bodach" comes from the Old Irish *botach*, meaning "serf" or "peasant," but it evolved into a derogatory term akin to "churl," "old man," or "clown." "Bodach" also derives from *bod* (tail or phallus) with the suffix *-ach*, suggesting a playfully crude origin.

Variations

Across Ireland, Scotland, and Wales, tales of the Bodach vary but often share common elements: He serves as a harbinger of death, and often, he is accused of stealing children and keeping them in his underground lair. This threatening image is still used to invoke fear and good behavior in some children in these areas.

The Bodach also embodies the tension between Celtic paganism and Christian reinterpretation. Originally linked to ancient deities, he became a symbol of fear and mischief in the Christian era. Recent interpretations portray the Bodach as a bogeyman to frighten children into obedience, and older legends link the name to mythic figures such as the Cailleach (the winter hag). In some stories, he is a persona taken on by the sea god Manannán Mac Lir.

The sea god story highlights the Bodach's mischievous side. Purely for the sake of amusement, the great sea god Manannán transformed himself into the Bodach and, carrying three spears in his hand, infiltrated a king's feast. He mocked the musicians brutally and then played a harp so beautifully that it healed all wounds and ailments in the hall. He tricked the king's guards into fighting and killing each other, only to restore them to life with a magical herb. The sea god also takes on the Bodach persona to toy with the Fianna in a story about a giant called Ironbones.

The Story You Need to Know

On the southwest coast of Ireland, a poor family gathered in their stone cottage to care for their ailing daughter Maura during the darkest days in the depths of winter. Shadows flickered across the stone walls in their small cottage as the fire devoured what little fuel they had to feed it. Maura's mother noticed a cold draft, and a chill ran up her spine. She turned to see a gaunt, hollow-eyed figure standing in the shadows. His long white hair framed his pale sagging skin and dark, lifeless eyes. She knew without asking that this was Bodach Glas—the Gray Churl.

He lifted a long, bony finger and pointed at the sickly child. The mother's breath shortened and cold sweat ran from her brow. She could do nothing. Her husband noticed the look of terror on her face, but when he followed her gaze, he saw nothing. In a gust of wind that nearly extinguished the fire, the Bodach vanished.

A sleepless night followed, and when the first rays of the winter sun lit up their home, Maura lay lifeless next to the embers of the dying fire. Her mother knew her death confirmed the Bodach's visit. Ever since, locals have kept salt in their hearths during winter, since all you need to stay safe from the Bodach is some salt. Throw it at him if you see him, or line the border of your home with salt to ensure safety from this malevolent spirit.

Despite evolving interpretations, the Bodach remains a figure that challenges the boundaries between life and death, good and evil, and mischief and malevolence. Whether as a grim herald or clever trickster, he reflects humanity's enduring fascination with the unknown.

Now You Know

During the Celtic Revival, the Bodach reemerged in literature. Writers like James Clarence Mangan and W.B. Yeats highlighted his trickster qualities, while Walter Scott referenced him in his historical novel *Waverley*. In modern works, such as Dean Koontz's Odd Thomas series, the Bodach appears as a death-omen shadow, blending ancient lore with contemporary storytelling.

ÁBHARTACH & THE BAOBHAN SÌTH

PRONUNCIATION: AV-ar-tok; BAH-van SITH

The Ábhartach and the Baobhan Sìth embody the supernatural predator in Celtic mythology. They are seen as early vampires, or the folkloric precursors to what we now know as modern vampires. Descriptions of these creatures lack many of the later specific traits associated with vampires, though—there are no coffins, garlic holds no power over them, and there is no real mention of sharp canines or any of that smoky romanticization that got mixed into vampire lore. In Celtic mythology, these creatures embody a primal fear of predatory, blood-drinking beings that rise from the dead seeking vengeance and/or sustenance.

Ábhartach was a short, cruel, undead Irish chieftain who rose multiple times from his grave, demanding blood from his village. The Baobhan Sìth was a Scottish Highlands faery who hunted alone or in groups, luring her victims with beauty, only to drain their life force. Together, these figures embody primal fears of the undead and the supernatural dangers of the night.

VARIATIONS

A later Irish folktale called the Dearg Due also plays with the themes of the undead enacting vengeance, where bloodless bodies were left in this woman's wake. In this tale, a beautiful, red-haired young woman (Dearg Due) was the victim of sustained abuse at the hands of her husband, the local lord. After her death, she was seen at the crossroads, embracing her husband and leaving him drained of blood. More people began to go missing, though it seemed that the Dearg Due had a preference for the blood of men who harmed women, linking her to ancient goddesses like the Morrígan and Danu.

THE STORY YOU NEED TO KNOW

Ábhartach ruled his people from a place called Slaghtaverty, Ireland, inspiring fear and hatred. He was a twisted, misshapen figure, his stature reflecting the malevolence of his nature. He practiced black magic and treated his wife with particular cruelty.

Eventually, the villagers rebelled against him, and a local hero called Cathain killed him. But to everyone's dismay, Ábhartach rose again, more bloodthirsty than before. This time, he walked into the village and demanded bowlfuls of the villagers' blood. Cathain killed him again, to no avail: The Ábhartach returned to life again.

Cathain sought the help of a druid, who explained that Ábhartach had become one of the undead. The undead had bottomless appetites that could never be appeased. Often, they would return to the home where they had lived when alive and demand food, eating ravenously until the family's resources were all consumed and driving them into poverty. The particular wickedness of the Ábhartach in life led to his demands for blood sacrifice. The druid said that only an ancient ritual could keep him from rising.

Cathain followed the druid's instructions, carving a sword from the wood of the yew tree to kill the Ábhartach, burying him upside down, and sealing the grave with a standing stone set vertically on top. The locals planted thorn trees all around the grave to enhance the protections, and the creature was trapped. The grave, now known as Slaghtaverty Dolmen, still stands as a warning against disturbing this restless spirit.

The Baobhan Sìth, a malevolent faery of the Scottish Highlands, hunts alone or in groups, preying on hunters with her deadly beauty. In one popular tale, four hunters settled down for the night, one wishing for female company. Four beautiful women appeared, joining them in a dance. But the women soon revealed their true nature as they clawed into the men to drink their blood. One man escaped to the woods, hiding until dawn (when the Baobhan Sìth retreated from sunlight, their greatest weakness). Iron tools or weapons are thought to ward off the Baobhan Sìth and are still considered essential for travelers in the Highlands.

Now You Know

Ábhartach and the Baobhan Sìth reflect ancient fears of undead forces and supernatural predators. Some suggest Ábhartach may have inspired Bram Stoker's *Dracula*, and his grave at Slaghtaverty Dolmen still holds fascination for local people. The Baobhan Sìth's allure, bloodlust, and vulnerability to iron connect her to broader Celtic lore about malevolent faery folk. From Ábhartach's bloodthirsty return to the Baobhan Sìth's deadly dance, these figures embody the consequences of human vulnerability meeting supernatural forces. The 2020 Netflix film *Boys from County Hell* draws on the legend of the Ábhartach and tells a story of the ancient grave being disrupted and the creature being released.

REDCAP

PRONUNCIATION: **RED**-cap
ALSO KNOWN AS: BLOODCAP, THE GOBLIN OF HERMITAGE CASTLE, POWRIE, DUNTER, FEAR DEARG, FAR DARRIG

Redcaps are terrifying goblins from Scottish folklore. Their "red caps" are that color because they're blood-soaked, and they are truly vicious, murderous creatures, said to die if their caps ever dry out. So they kill at every opportunity, and with relish, in order to resoak their caps in the blood of their victims. They often dwell in old, ruined castles on the England–Scotland border where ancient atrocities have taken place.

Redcaps are evil, goblin-like faeries that embody a relentless, malevolent spirit. They haunt old battlefields as a reminder of past violence. While they possess immense strength, their weakness is anything religious. Presenting a crucifix or repeating holy scripture provides a defense against them, and the Redcap disappears in a flash of flame if so thwarted.

VARIATIONS

The term "Redcap" is also found in Wales but refers to benevolent faeries who wore green clothing and innocently sported red caps that were presumably dyed with perfectly normal plant dyes and not fresh blood.

Another kindly Redcap exists in tales from Perthshire in central Scotland, taking residence in the upper floors of Grandtully Castle. These Redcaps offer the local people protection and good fortune rather than terror and death.

Along the Northumbrian–Scottish border, Redcaps may be referred to as Powries or Dunters and are less malicious. The Powrie's screech warns of misfortune to come. Other malicious creatures share characteristics with the Redcap, but without the sheer glee of killing the Redcap portrays.

The Fear Dearg (Red Man; also called Far Darrig) of Irish folklore is a similarly evil spirit. Akin to the devil, the image of a Fear Dearg is never a good thing. Offering help for a heavy price, the Fear Dearg is a sinister trickster who will steal your most prized possession and take your ignorance for granted. Especially associated with Samhain (Halloween), the trick this creature plays might take the life of your loved ones.

The Story You Need to Know

The Redcap is an unusual fae, as it seems to have been cast out from the faery realm for its malicious habits. It cannot use the magic of the Otherworld and is bound to use iron weapons and wear iron boots. It is cannibalistic by nature and devours human and Otherworldly kin alike.

Redcaps are described in countless tales as short, thick-set old men with elongated features. For example, they have long, skinny fingers with sharp claws at the tips, akin to an eagle's talons. The Redcap clutches an iron pikestaff or scythe in one hand and wears heavy iron boots. His large, pointed, prominent teeth appear in a wide grin, and his sunken, fiery red eyes pierce into anyone unlucky enough to meet him. Matted gray hair (which is clotted with the blood dripping from his wet red cap) frames the mottled gray skin of his face. The red cap is, of course, a grisly feature he must maintain, as the cap's brightness provides his malevolent lifeforce. In short: It's a truly terrifying creature to behold.

These creatures lurk in castles with histories of violence, launching stones at unfortunate travelers seeking shelter in the deserted castles near the borders of Scotland and England. Once killed, their victims' blood refreshes the Redcaps' headgear, which is their defining mark and source of power.

Redcaps are nearly invulnerable to brute strength alone and, despite wearing iron boots, are quick enough to hunt down any fleeing victims that happen to cross their lairs. Holding up a Bible or crucifix or quoting scripture can repel them, causing them to disappear in a flash of fire, leaving behind only a large tooth as a mark of their demise.

One famous tale centers on Robin Redcap, a goblin servant to the cruel Border Lord at Hermitage Castle (Lord William de Soulis), who entered into an evil pact with this Redcap in exchange for Otherworldly powers. Together, they tormented the surrounding region with unchecked violence. As his servant, Robin Redcap seemed to give the lord magical powers of his own, rendering the Lord at Hermitage invulnerable to normal weapons.

Eventually, the local people rose up in rebellion. They drove the Redcap off by chanting scripture, then attempted to hang their evil lord. When that failed because of the lingering influence of the demonic Redcap, they dragged him to a nearby stone circle and boiled him alive in a cauldron of lead.

He might have been better off being hanged, but evil pacts rarely end well in folklore.

Now You Know

Redcaps represent the haunting legacy of violence between Scotland and England. They serve as a reminder of the thousands of years of war and strife and the bandits and marauders who were once so prominent between surrounding hills. Their blood-red caps are reminders of their brutality, while their vulnerability to religious symbols underscores the era's belief in faith as a shield against evil. Their presence in abandoned castles, spaces between human habitation and ruin, further accentuates their eerie reputation and connection to the shadowed past.

Folklorist William Henderson gathered many stories of Redcaps and similar solitary creatures. *The Iron Man* by Ted Hughes, *The Darkest Part of the Forest* by Holly Black, and The Spiderwick Chronicles series by Tony DiTerlizzi and Holly Black feature creatures reminiscent of the Redcap. They also inspire creatures in The Witcher and Dark Souls video game series.

THE DULLAHAN

PRONUNCIATION: DUL-A-HAN
ALSO KNOWN AS: FENYW HEB UN PEN, HEADLESS HORSEMEN/-WOMEN

The Dullahan is a ghostly headless horseman who strikes fear into the hearts of lonely travelers on the road. Whether seen as a vengeful ghost or the servant of a death god, this terrifying monster appears on isolated roads to collect the souls of those he marks for death. Carrying his severed head in one hand, wielding a whip made from the vertebrae of a spine, and riding a great black horse, he strikes a fearsome image. Unlike other creatures who merely foretell death, the Dullahan is actually a relentless hunter and collector of souls.

VARIATIONS

In Wales and Cornwall, the headless horseman is a headless horse-*woman*, astride a headless horse. In the Welsh tradition, her name is Fenyw heb un pen (the headless woman), and she rides Ceffyl heb un pen (the headless horse). She haunted Bryn Hall in southeast Wales until a grave was discovered to contain the body of the Lord of Bryn Hall's illegitimate child, buried near the hall.

In Scotland, the rider is named Ewan "The Headless" MacLaine and foretells death in his own MacLaine clan. Ewan was a warrior who ignored the Bean Nighe washing his clothes before a battle. He was beheaded in the fight but managed to pull himself onto his horse and ride away before he died.

THE STORY YOU NEED TO KNOW

The trope of the headless horseman has become iconic across Europe, and there are specific tales of the equestrian death rider in Ireland, Scotland, and Wales. In Ireland, pre-Christian King Tigernmas was said to have made a bargain for fair harvests with a brutal pagan deity called Crom Cruach. Little is known about Crom Cruach—except that his name means "bent, crooked, stooped"—though there are hints that he was either worshipped as a god of harvest and death or that he was a last pagan holdout, a chieftain who refused to convert to Christianity. Some say that the Dullahan is a mere ghost of a foreign soldier, but others say that he is a servant of Crom Cruach, sent to collect the souls he was promised in exchange for fair harvests.

An unwary traveler out after dark, particularly at certain times of the year when the veil is thin, might hear the heavy hoofbeats of the Dullahan. The Dullahan can see for miles in every direction, and can hold his severed head up high to get a better vantage point. He can also see through walls and pass through any gate, lock, or door. Astride his great horse, he wields a whip made out of the vertebrae of a human spine. The flesh of his severed head sags, rotted and loose, and glows with an eerie light.

The Dullahan speaks very little. In fact, he can only speak the name of the one whose soul he is about to collect. If he is ever witnessed by someone whose soul is not claimed, he lashes out with his terrible whip, blinding them in one eye.

As with most of the malevolent creatures of the Otherworld, however, the best defense against the Dullahan is to not encounter him in the first place—by avoiding lonely stretches of road when the veil is thin. If a person does meet the creature on the road and hears their own name spoken, there is little to be done.

In fact, the only way to temporarily chase the Dullahan away is by using gold. The creature has a terrible fear of the rare soft metal and can be driven off by the smallest amount. But this is a mere warding and not a full banishing. Nothing can truly put the Dullahan down, and he will return time and time again, hunting his quarry until the night he can catch them unawares.

Unlike most creatures of the Otherworld, the Dullahan is not slowed by iron bars or closed doors. Once he has spoken a name, he will stop at nothing to collect that soul.

Now You Know

The Dullahan is regarded as the probable inspiration behind Washington Irving's "The Legend of Sleepy Hollow" and other tales of headless horsemen. Whether known as the Dullahan, Ewan, or the Welsh Fenyw heb un pen, the headless rider is a figure that strikes terror into those who hear its ominous approach.

The Dullahan has no true weaknesses but is rumored to be deterred by gold, making it a rare commodity worth carrying if you wish to evade his wrath. His iconic haunting presence continues to gallop through modern culture, appearing in video games such as *Assassin's Creed III*, *Assassin's Creed Rogue*, *The Elder Scrolls V: Skyrim*, *Roblox*, and *World of Warcraft*, among others.

KELPIES & EACH UISCE

PRONUNCIATION: KELL-PEE; EA-K UISH-KA

There are many creatures that lurk in the murky waters of the Celtic islands. The deep, murky depths are home to many of the frightening shades of our shared imaginative realm. Scottish water horses go by two names: the Each Uisce and the Kelpie. The Each Uisce (meaning "water horse") lurks in lochs and is reputed to be even more vicious than the saltwater horse known as the Kelpie. A Kelpie is a shape-shifting monster that lures the unwary to their doom, either in the form of a beautiful horse or a beautiful man.

VARIATIONS

There are many similar tales of water horses in Celtic mythology. For example, the Nuggle haunts the rivers of Orkney, a group of islands off the northeast coast of Scotland. Lochs and streams on Scotland's Shetland Islands are said to be inhabited by the Shoopiltee, and the Isle of Man is home to the Cabbyl-Ushtey. The Welsh counterpart is the Ceffyl Dŵr, with the one distinction that it mostly seems to inhabit mountain pools and lakes, but similarly lures and drowns its victims.

Waterways are generally considered passages to the Otherworld in Celtic folklore, liminal places full of power, potential, and danger. While these horse-like creatures disguise their savage nature behind a pleasing facade, the fearsome Irish Oilliphéist is as nasty as it looks, haunting the dark depths of pools and carving the courses of great rivers with its

movement. The Oilliphéist is a kind of water-dragon or serpent that lives in lakes and bodies of water. Many of Ireland's most important rivers, such as the River Lee, are said to have been carved by an Oilliphéist as it fled from a great hero or saint.

THE STORY YOU NEED TO KNOW

The Kelpie often appears as a beautiful white horse grazing near a body of water, usually a lake or a seashore. When an adventurous youth attempts to ride the horse, they find themselves stuck fast to the horse's back. Anyone who attempts to pull them off is similarly stuck. Once the creature has lured as many people as it can, it races at top speed for the lake, diving below the water and drowning its unfortunate riders. Such an encounter can only be survived if one cuts off whichever limb is magically attached to the Kelpie.

Sometimes, Kelpies appear as handsome young men who seduce maidens and eventually carry them off to their watery lairs.

Usually, this is the end of the Kelpie story, with a warning to be wary of strange horses and strange men. A Scottish story expands on this basic tale and offers multiple variations. At a great gathering of seven kings from Ireland and Scotland, the seven sons of the kings went out hunting while their elders talked. At the end of the day, a single warrior returned with his hand severed at the wrist and a terrible story to tell. The princes had come across a beautiful white horse and were determined to ride it; to their delight, they found that there was room on its back for all seven. Once the princes had all mounted up, the Kelpie (for of course it was a Kelpie) raced to the shore and dove beneath a whirlpool. The warrior managed to get a hand onto its flank but could not dislodge any of the princes, and he had to cut his own hand off to escape.

One of the kings' druids set about making a spell to try and free the princes from the Kelpie's grasp, but he had little hope for their rescue. Meanwhile, a young woman who lived near the shore was enjoying the company of her handsome new lover. His dark hair never seemed to fully dry, and he would not come into her home, but the first time she'd met him, she had wiped the tears from his eyes and fallen deeply in love with him.

One evening, she fell asleep in his arms on the beach after making love but woke late in the night. To her shock, the moonlight revealed the true form of the Kelpie, which was neither a beautiful white horse nor a beautiful young man, but a horse-like creature of seaweed and sharp bones. She fled, but the love spell that had snared her through the Kelpie's tears twisted back on its maker, and the creature became enamored with her.

Hearing the news from the castle, she realized that this Kelpie must have been the same one that had taken the kings' sons. She demanded that it release the princes before she would consider seeing it again. The lovelorn Kelpie complied, though the king's druid got the credit for the rescue. The woman went back to her own life, content to know the truth for herself.

Now You Know

Superstitions around strange creatures lurking in the dark, murky depths of lakes may have influenced the rise of the more recent belief in the Loch Ness Monster. If that does turn out to be a Kelpie, cryptid-hunters would be well advised to steer clear.

Modern references to Kelpies appear in several works. The towering *Kelpies* sculptures in Falkirk, Scotland, created by Andy Scott, honor these magical water horses in Scotland. The 2007 film *The Water Horse: Legend of the Deep* and Maggie Stiefvater's novel *The Scorpio Races* draw on the dark and dangerous allure of this legend. Even the TV series *Outlander* references these legends in the episode "Both Sides Now," blending Scottish folklore with modern drama.

SELKIES/MERROWS

PRONUNCIATION: **SEL**-keys; **MER**-rows
ALSO KNOWN AS: Seal-Woman, Seal-Man, Sea-Maiden

Seals are wonderful creatures that are seen in their hundreds on the shores of Scotland, Wales, and Ireland, moving swiftly in the water (and awkwardly on land). People fishing can even befriend seals with regular offerings of fish thrown from their boats. Their human-like eyes peering curiously from the water can capture the imagination.

In the Scottish islands of Orkney, the word for seal is "selkie." The Selkies of folklore are seals in the sea but humans on land, and their beauty is irresistible to any mortal who sees them. Selkies can remove their skin and transform into human form, captivating mortals and singing haunting melodies. Once the Selkie skin is donned again, they transform into seal form and return to the sea.

VARIATIONS

In Ireland, the alluring sea creature goes by the name of "Merrow," as told in the story "The Lady of Gollerus." Merrows are green-skinned and humanoid—they do not change shape but instead use a red cap to breathe underwater. (The cap functions similarly to a Selkie's skin and bears no relation to the mythological Redcap figures.)

THE STORY YOU NEED TO KNOW

In most Selkie stories, a mortal falls in love with this Otherworldly creature, and it rarely ends well. The most common story is that of the Selkie Wife (which directly parallels Irish stories such as "The Lady of Gollerus"). The landscape, location, and minor details vary, but most stories go something like this:

One night, while the moon is full and bright, a fisherman walks by the shore, pondering his loneliness and his lack of marital prospects. He hears sweet singing rising over the waves and goes to find its source. From a hiding place in the rocks, he sees a number of Selkies singing and dancing in the moonlight and is captivated by their beauty and song. Thinking quickly, he snatches up one of the seal-skins discarded on the beach and hides it under his coat. At dawn, all of the Selkies but one retrieve their skins and slip back under the waves as seals once more. The lone Selkie searches in vain—she cannot find her skin.

The fisherman approaches the terrified woman and, acting innocent, offers her his hand and his coat and invites her back to his home (all while hiding the fact that he has her stolen skin). She follows him, comforted by his apparent kindness. He feeds and clothes her, and while she sleeps by the fire, he finds a special hiding place for her Selkie skin.

The two eventually get married. Now that he has a wife to cook, clean, and mend the fishing nets, the fisherman's fortunes improve greatly. Soon the pair have children and are content—for the most part. Sometimes the Selkie wife pines for her lost life under the sea. This yearning is especially strong under the full moon, when she stares longingly at the waves.

One fateful day, the fisherman leaves home for longer than usual. By some trick of fortune, either dislodged by the children at play or by an unusually thorough spring cleaning, the Selkie Wife finds her skin. As soon as the skin is back in her hands, she kisses her children goodbye and leaves for the freedom of the ocean, never to be seen again, though her mortal husband and children search for her.

Originally, these stories were meant to warn men not to marry outsiders for fear of their "strange" ways. Modern retellings focus on the Selkie woman's autonomy through her ability to escape and rediscover her true self after a tumultuous, or coercive, relationship.

Though the main story focuses on Selkie women, some stories of Selkie men do exist. For example, Selkie men were often blamed for unexpected pregnancies when there was no father to be found. Their allure could explain away the woman's unwarranted desire. Children born with webbed feet or fingers were assumed to have Selkie blood.

Now You Know

The intrinsic association and romanticization of the ocean and its beautiful creatures is encapsulated by our obsession with these people from the sea. Straddling both life in the sea and either a tragic or brief time on land, these half-human, half-fishlike creatures captured our imagination long before Disney's *The Little Mermaid*, as merpeople have existed in Celtic lore for as long as we can recall.

The Selkie has appeared in many films over the years—most notably *The Secret of Roan Inish* and Colin Farrell's *Ondine*—as well as episodes of the television shows *Supernatural*, *The Dresden Files*, and *Gravity Falls*. The Merrows appear as aquatic ogres in Dungeons & Dragons games, and as a type of merfolk in the card game Magic: The Gathering. They also exist in the Harry Potter spinoff series Fantastic Beasts, and in the video game *Puyo Puyo*.

CATH PALUG

PRONUNCIATION: KATH **PAH**-LOOG (WALES)
ALSO KNOWN AS: CAT OF PALUG, PALUG'S CAT

Cath Palug is a monstrous feline from Welsh mythology, known for its immense size, ferocious appetite, and confrontations with legendary heroes. The name "Cath Palug" translates to "Palug's Cat," with "Palug" possibly connected to the Welsh word for "scratching," "claw," or "plague." These translations suggest that this cat was no mere house cat, but rather a fearsome creature, malevolent in nature, and representing the mystery and the terror of the wild. The tale of Cath Palug is scattered across various fragments of Welsh folklore and was later revived by Arthurian legend.

THE STORY YOU NEED TO KNOW

This water cat's story starts with…a pig. Henwen was a magical sow, a female pig, in Wales. Pigs were believed to be a gift from the Otherworld (see Pryderi's entry), and Henwen was carefully tended by her swineherd, Coll, who was one of the Three Powerful Swineherds of the British Isles, no less. Swineherds held a surprisingly high status in Celtic society.

A prophecy said that the offspring of Henwen would cause three terrible plagues. (In Wales, it's always three.) The pig was chased across the country, but it was too late. She gave birth to three creatures, all of which became scourges, as predicted. The first two were an eagle and a wolf, but two powerful men decided to adopt these extremely macho creatures as mascots. Neither of them fared well, but they kept those plagues confined to their own households, so nobody else cared very much.

Henwen wasn't all bad. She was also the progenitor of wheat, barley, rye, and bees—which were all extremely helpful to the humans who feared her.

Apparently Coll managed to catch up with Henwen in Llanfair (in northwest Wales), just after she'd given birth at Black Rock to a black kitten. He assumed that since it wasn't a grain or an insect, it was probably another one of her terrible beasts, and cast the newborn kitten into the sea, assuming it would drown.

It did not.

Turns out, the kitten was a water cat, so it swam. It swam across the Menai Strait, the sea between mainland Wales and the Isle of Anglesey, where it was found and then raised by the unsuspecting sons of Palug. At first, it grew like a normal kitten, but people started to get concerned when it kept growing...and growing. Cath Palug grew to a monstrous size, with claws as large as swords and teeth the size of spears. The giant cat began hunting wild game and even preyed on humans, and began terrorizing the region. The situation became known as one of the Three Great Oppressions of Anglesey.

Descriptions of the cat varied, possibly because anyone seeing it was trying very hard to avoid being eaten. Some say it was black, others say it was spotted. Most said nothing, as they lay in the belly of the beast.

Cath Palug became such a problem that King Arthur himself sent an army, led by Sir Cai (or Kay), to face the beast. During the battle, 180 warriors were killed and eaten by the beastly kitty. The poem that tells this story ends with Cai facing off against the monstrous cat with a polished shield—but the final verses are missing, as if torn away by a resentful cat. And so, we can never know who was victorious.

Other tales tell of King Arthur taking matters into his own hands. He brought an army to the foot of the mountain Cath Palug was reported to be using as its lair. But Arthur wanted no more bloodshed, so he hiked the hill himself, determined to face the creature alone.

Giant ears heard him and four clawed paws landed lightly in front of the great king. With a flick of its tail, Cath Palug launched itself at Arthur. Snapping teeth and sliding claws came at Arthur fast and hard. His bright, brilliant shield barely saved his skin as he ducked and dodged, swivelling and diving away from the cat's deadly blows.

His sword came down on the clawing beast and cut the sharp weapons from its paws. It hissed and arched and struck again faster than Arthur could contend with, and Cath Palug's claw dug into his shoulder. But as it picked him up and brought him toward its hungry mouth, Arthur struck his sword in under its chin and up through the roof of its foul-smelling mouth. The day was won, but Arthur would later admit that this was the greatest fear he had ever felt.

Cath Palug's tale blends the themes of chaos, heroism, survival, and the struggle between civilization and the wild. Its association with King Arthur himself underscores its significance as a formidable adversary in Celtic and Arthurian mythology. Truth will never get in the way of a good story, though: Cath Palug's story is inconclusive and still open to interpretation, and this tale is a combination of various sources into one narrative. There is also a local legend in Scotland that claims a cracked boulder beside Dunbar Castle was broken by one of the claws of Cath Palug as it fought against the people there, perhaps showing that the cat had ranged over territories far from its home base.

Now You Know

Anime lovers will be delighted to know that *The Seven Deadly Sins* series draws heavily from this tale in its fourth season and reimagines Cath Palug as the bringer of Chaos against a very young-looking Arthur.

In France, there is a legend of a creature of identical description known as Chapalu. When it faced King Arthur in battle, the cat was victorious. This legend has left a geographical legacy, with landmarks like Mont du Chat and Col du Chat near the French Alps in France commemorating its mythic battles.

CÙ-SÌTH, CŴN ANNWN, THE BLACK DOG & WOLFHOUNDS

PRONUNCIATION: COO-SITH; COON-ANN-OON

The Cù-Sìth is the great "faery hound" and one of the most feared creatures in Celtic lore. These giant, malevolent spectral hounds are deeply tied to the Aos Sí (faery folk) and their wild hunt. They haunt the Scottish Highlands and Irish moors and make their lairs in coastal caves. They are the size of bulls, with shaggy dark green or luminous emerald fur, and burning yellow firelike eyes, visible long before the silent hunters are ever heard. Some have flat braided tails, and others are described as having long, flowing tails that coil over and above them.

Legends warn of their three terrifying howls, each a chilling omen of death, usually for an unsuspecting traveler. The first blood-curdling howl signals to flee, the second brings terror, and the third seals one's fate. If a traveler hears the third, death is certain, often from sheer fright before the Cù-Sìth arrives to devour their soul. Pregnant women were especially vulnerable, as folklore claimed the Cù-Sìth kidnapped them to nurse faery children, stealing their milk for the people of the Otherworld.

Variations

The many variations of these magical hounds in Celtic lore portray the intangible yet profoundly beautiful and powerful bond between humans and hounds. Whether due to outright fear of their wild savagery, a loving connection, or simply respect, hounds in Celtic folklore demand attention. The Cù-Sìth appears in several regional tales.

- On the island of Tiree, a man encountered a sleeping green hound in daylight but escaped unscathed. Skeptics later found giant paw prints too large to be natural. Later, the lair of the dog was found by a shepherd who sheltered in a coastal cave during a storm and discovered a litter of green pups. Fearing their mother's return, he fled. He heard two howls but he managed to hide in an abandoned hut before the third and final howl sealed his fate. His flock vanished, but he and his dogs survived unharmed.

- On the Isle of Lewis, a farmer once found a giant tooth thought to belong to the Cù-Sìth. It had healing properties when placed in water and was handed down as a family heirloom for generations.

- The Black Dog in Irish folklore is massive and shadowy. It appears on lonely roads, often blocking a traveler's path. It is always an omen of misfortune or death and never a welcome sight in the dark.

- The Cŵn Annwn of Welsh mythology are white hounds with red ears who serve as the hunting pack of Arawn, the ruler of Annwn, the Welsh Otherworld. They guide souls to the afterlife, feed on corpses, or act as omens of death. The Cŵn Annwn are also thought to have special hunting grounds on the mountain of Cadair Idris in Wales.

Not all the hounds in Celtic myth are terrible. The legend of Gelert is a tale of loyalty and tragic misjudgment. Llywelyn the Last, the prince of

Wales starting in 1258, returned from a hunt to find his faithful hound Gelert standing over his child's cradle, bloodied. Assuming the worst, the prince killed Gelert, only to discover a slain wolf beneath the cradle with the child safe inside. Gelert had saved the child. Overcome with grief, Llywelyn buried his loyal companion, and a site ("Gelert's Grave") in the tiny Welsh village of Beddgelert stands as a testament to this tragedy.

The well-known Irish tale of how Cúchulainn got his name (Cúchulainn literally means "the hound of Culann") was earned when the boy, then named Setanta, killed a supernaturally huge and vicious hound that guarded the lands of the blacksmith Culann (see Cúchulainn's entry for the full story). This hound was descended from a fearsome hound that had terrorized the countryside. Three pups were found after it was killed: a white pup that went to a chieftain in Leinster (and caused a war when both Ulster and Connaught tried to claim it), a brindled pup that went to the blacksmith Culann to be his guard dog, and a black pup that went to the south to fade into the mists and become an omen of death.

THE STORY YOU NEED TO KNOW

On a dark and dreadful night on the island of Benbecula, on the west coast of Scotland, where the clan of the MacDonalds once ruled, two men sat around the fireside heating their hands and wishing that the early spring were warmer. It was their duty that night to protect the newly born calves. As they sat guard, they told each other stories of the creatures in the Highlands.

Just as one tale ended and they were feeling particularly spooked by the sound of the rain lashing on the dark earth outside, they saw two giant hounds, the Cù-Sìth, leap from the forest and run straight toward them. As the firelight landed on these immense, spectral hounds, they noticed that both dogs were collared in a strange metal, featuring jewels and precious stones of many colors.

The Cù-Sìth approached, their snarling mouths showing yellow fangs, and the men were paralyzed with fear. Suddenly, a voice came out of the forest and the giant green ears of the hounds twitched to listen. The commanding voice called the hounds away, back to the slender fae who were moving through the countryside.

The Cù-Sìth turned and went back to the forest toward the disembodied voice. Once the two men had regained their wits about them, they both went out into the darkness of the night. They saw large paw prints in the mud and tracked them into the forest.

The Aos Sí (the faerie host, often seen on the move in this way in folklore) walked in procession on horseback, with spears in hand, each member holding a hawk on their shoulder and accompanied by a hound, or Cú-Sìth, beside them. The Aos Sí were on the hunt. The two men hid from view and witnessed them marching through the forest and continuing out west over the sea, in search of an unknown prey. After they were sure to be a safe distance away, and only because custom decrees, the two men wished them luck on their hunt and returned, glad of the tale they could tell at the next fireside, and grateful that the faery host had chosen not to hunt men on that night.

Now You Know

The Cù-Sìth's spectral presence in folklore reflects humanity's fascination with death, savagery, and loyalty. These figures also resonate in popular culture, inspiring figures like the Grim in *Harry Potter and the Prisoner of Azkaban* and the terrifying creature in *The Hound of the Baskervilles*. Their silent steps, glowing eyes, and harbingering howls continue to evoke awe and fear today.

FAOLADH/ WULVERS/ GWRGI GARWLWYD

PRONUNCIATION: FWAY-LAA; WUL-VERS; GOR-GEE GAG-GLE-RIOD
ALSO KNOWN AS: WEREWOLVES; MAN-DOG; THE ROUGH-GRAY MAN-DOG

Celtic lore is rich with tales of shape-shifting and animal transformation. One creature that is a constant source of awe and inspiration is the wolf. *Faoladh* is the Irish term for "werewolf," although there is no connection to forced transformations triggered by the moon. The physical transformation from a human into a wolf could be done on command by some, or through dream work by others. In those cases, the human body was left behind as if in a state of sleep, and the mind became connected to the body of a wolf. Celtic wolf lore laid some of the foundations for modern-day werewolves, but the whole "full moon" thing was never part of it.

VARIATIONS

Numerous variations and stories across Celtic culture illustrate the symbolic power of wolves as both protectors and destroyers. This dual identity in wolf lore encapsulates the tension between civilization and savagery, and reason and instinct—presenting a more nuanced view of these beasts, which are usually associated with wildness and savagery.

PART 3: Creatures & Monsters

The Wulvers in Scotland were half-man, half-wolf and were generally good-natured warriors who protected the natural world. Permanently in wolf-man form, the Wulver is not a shape-shifter but rather a benevolent creature who aids lost travelers and leaves food for the poor. This depiction offers insight into the kinder aspects of werewolf lore, reflecting a local culture that embodies generosity and support.

In later Irish folklore, the wolf form became a common way that holy men cursed recalcitrant pagans. A priest was out walking in the woods one day in the medieval Irish kingdom of Ossory and was approached by a wolf with a human voice. The wolf asked him to come and perform the last rites on his partner. The priest obeyed, out of fear or curiosity—or both. When he met the she-wolf, she removed her wolf skin to reveal her human form as an old lady, and the priest gave her last rites. The wolves told the priest their story. A holy man had placed the people of Ossory under a curse due to their refusal to change their pagan ways. Every seven years, a man and woman had to be chosen to take a wolf form. After telling the story, the she-wolf died, and the other wolf stalked back into the woods, howling his human sorrow into the night.

Further variations of these tales can be found with subtle differences, such as where the wolves talk with human voices, or seem to shift form. A folktale from Wicklow tells of how a farmer's herd of cattle went missing. He had previously helped a wolf with an injured paw. When he went out to search for his cattle, he was invited into a strange little cottage by a man who seemed oddly familiar to him. Though everything appeared normal, he kept getting glimpses out of the corner of his eye, seeing his hosts as wolves and the cozy cottage as a den under the tree roots. He told his story, and his hosts apologized for the misunderstanding, saying they hadn't known those were *his* cattle. After waking up, he found a new, better herd of cattle waiting for him at home, likely stolen for him by the remorseful wolves in repayment of his earlier kindness.

A vicious Celtic werewolf also appears in Welsh Arthurian legend. Gwrgi Garwlwyd, known as the "Rough-Gray Man-Dog," is the champion of a group of warriors called the *cinbin* (dog-headed warriors) who fought near Edinburgh. Gwrgi Garwlwyd was initially one of Arthur's men but became a vicious and bloodthirsty killer who murdered a man a day and two on Saturday so that he could take a break on Sunday. He was eventually defeated in battle.

The Story You Need to Know

The Daughters of Airitech were three Otherworldly sisters who transformed into Faoladh (werewolves) every year and slaughtered neighboring sheep and calves. They came through an Otherworldly portal in Crúachan Aí (in the west of Ireland), known as Oweynagat, a cave formation that can still be visited today and is usually associated with the Morrígan.

They came every year at Samhain, or modern-day Halloween, when the veil between worlds was at its thinnest and their magic was strongest. As wolves, they loved to cause havoc among the local herds. The sisters seemed to think of it as a game, oblivious to the annual terror they were causing the locals.

A hero of the Fianna called Caoilte came to help. He asked a local harper, Cas Corach, for help. Cas Corach perched beside the mouth of the cave at Oweynagat and played music to see if the wolves would be soothed by it. Sure enough, they came to listen. The plan was formed.

The following night Caoilte watched closely, spear in hand, and Cas Corach played to the she-wolves again. This time Cas Corach encouraged them to turn into their human form, as they would surely enjoy music more this way. The three sisters agreed and transformed in front of his eyes, sitting elbow to elbow, smiling up at him as his fingers moved swiftly over strings.

Caoilte moved fast. He drove his spear ruthlessly through the three Daughters of Airitech, showing no remorse. He killed them with one deadly blow, joining them together "like a skein of thread" connected between one spear. Though he saved the area from the scourge that had plagued them for years, he did so by destroying the magic of these three sisters forever, bringing protection to the people at the cost of driving a little more mystery and wonder out of the world.

The connections between wolves and Irish culture go back a long way. There are some accounts of ancient Celtic warriors wearing wolfskins as a way of connecting to the animals and the land. The word "wolf" in Irish, *mac tíre*, means "son of the land," and there were wolves in the Celtic Archipelago up until 1786, when the last wolf in Ireland was killed. The last wolf in England was killed much earlier, in the fourteenth century, so Ireland became particularly associated with wolves and was sometimes called "the land of the wolf."

Now You Know

In modern media, these shape-shifting figures continue to inspire narratives, from the protective Irish Faoladh to the benevolent Wulver, influencing portrayals of heroic or gentle werewolves. Popular culture, including television shows like *Teen Wolf* and films like *The Secret of Kells*, echoes themes from Celtic lore, showcasing werewolves as mysterious beings straddling the line between protector and monster.

The transportation of a person's mind into the mind of a beast comes up in fantasy literature by Terry Pratchett, in his Granny Weatherwax character, and in George R. R. Martin's A Song of Ice and Fire book series, where it is called "warging." The Oscar-nominated animation *Wolfwalkers* is set in Kilkenny, Ireland, where the ancient kingdom of Ossory was.

PART 3: Creatures & Monsters 131

FINNBENNACH & THE DONN CÚAILNGE

Pronunciation: FINN-ban-ack; DON CU-al-ne
Also Known As: the Bulls; Finnbennach is also called the White-Horned Bull of Crúachan Aí and the Donn Cúailnge is also called the Brown Bull of Cooley; The Swineherds: Rucht and Friuch

At the center of the Ulster Cycle collection of stories lies the epic *Táin Bó Cúailnge—The Cattle Raid of Cooley*. At the heart of that tale is the surprisingly complex backstory of two extraordinary creatures: the magical bulls whose rivalry drives the overarching conflict. The Connaught Bull, Finnbennach (also known as the White-Horned Bull of Crúachan Aí), and the Ulster Bull, the Donn Cúailnge (also known as the Brown Bull of Cooley), are no ordinary animals. They are monstrous, Otherworldly beings whose mere presence instigates this tragic war saga.

Their stories stretch back much further than the *Táin*. Once part of the Tuatha Dé Danann, their forms and fates are shaped and re-shaped by their own godlike abilities and very human stubbornness. Though their final physical forms are of bulls, they are far more than normal cattle—they are symbols of pride, power, and the devastating consequences of rivalry gone wrong. Their legendary battle spans lifetimes, as they change their shape to continuously challenge each other, leaving only destruction in their wake.

The Story You Need to Know

Long before the mortal battles of the Ulster Cycle, the godlike people known as the Tuatha Dé Danann ruled Ireland. The king of Munster, Bodhbh Dearg, and the king of Connaught, Ochall Ochne, each had a swineherd in his employ. It was their job to fatten their kings' pigs all year before they were slaughtered for meat. The swineherds' names were Rucht (meaning "bristle") of Connaught and Friuch (meaning "grunt") of Munster. They accompanied one another whenever they had a chance, and they fattened their pigs together in the bountiful forests, sharing in the good years. During this pleasant activity, and since they had the same interests, they became best friends.

People started to compare the two, claiming one king's swine were more succulent and well looked after than the other king's pigs. People began to pit them against each other, and so the former friendship turned to rivalry, and then hatred. First, Friuch cast a spell on Rucht's herd, so they did not fatten no matter how much they gorged. They wasted to skin and bone. Rucht lost his position as the king's swineherd and was cast out in disgrace, so he cast the same spell against Friuch's herd, with similar results.

The fight then turned physical. At a feast in Munster at Bodhbh Dearg's keep, thrown to welcome Ochall Ochne, the two swineherds disguised themselves as *fian* warriors, loyal to no king, and leaped at one another. The striking of their blades cast sparks that caught ablaze, and the fighting spread like wildfire until the hall was on the brink of war. But each was as good a fighter as the other, in every way.

They shifted their forms, continuing to fight. They became hawks who fought so loudly and fiercely over the kings' halls in Connaught and Munster that no one there could get a wink of sleep. They became sea monsters and battled in the ocean until the very waves turned red. They turned into shadow phantoms, battling in silhouette on the walls, and were so fearsome a sight that any who saw them were struck dead with fear. Eventually, they turned into tiny eels and tried to twist around each other.

But no matter what form they chose, they could not get the better of one another, and as eels they were too tiny to stand up against the force of the current. They were swept away. Perhaps they were pulled through time, or perhaps they lived as eels, unconscious of their former lives, for centuries. Whatever the way, both eels were swallowed at the same time, one by a cow in Connaught, and the other by a cow in Cooley. In the bellies of the cows, they changed again, becoming bull calves who had no memory of their past lives.

These bulls grew so huge and powerful it was said that ten men could play hurling (a traditional Irish game) on their backs. In a society that saw cattle as wealth, they were more precious than jewels. It was on their account that the great Cattle Raid of Cooley was fought. Thousands of lives were lost, displaced, and destroyed by that war.

When the Brown Bull of Cooley was driven back to Connaught, he smelled his old rival's scent on the wind. Whether they remembered everything, or whether they were driven by instinct, no one can say. But the Bulls fought with a ferocity that drove scars into the landscape of northern Connaught that remain there to this day. Anyone who got too close was trampled to death, and the sounds of their battle woke every babe in Ireland.

Their fight lasted for days until at last the Brown Bull caught the White-Horned in a wild swing and ripped out his throat with the tip of his horn. The Brown Bull picked up his rival's body on his horns and began a victory lap around Ireland, bellowing his victory to the skies. But when he came to the hills of Cooley, where he had been born as a bull, the Brown Bull's heart swelled with pride...and it burst, killing him instantly.

The Celtic Otherworld can feel so close at hand with the godlike beings still out there today, as creatures or rivers, changed in shape, in hiding, or in forgetting, in the forms of birds, or stags, or creatures in the sea. The sorcery among the Tuatha Dé Danann seems to have been so common that all had access to shape-shifting powers, so who knows how many more are still out there.

RED DRAGON/ Y DDRAIG GOCH

Pronunciation: uh-DRAI-g GOHKH
Also Known As: The Welsh Dragon; Emblem of Wales

Y Ddraig Goch, the heroic and enduring Red Dragon of Welsh mythology, stands as a powerful symbol of the strength, spirit, and resilience of the Welsh people. Deeply rooted in mythology, these elemental creatures of fire, water, earth, and air (they can spit fire, fly in the air, and live underwater or under the earth) came to represent strength, power, wisdom, and survival against adversity—qualities highly prized by the leaders of the warring Celtic tribes. Over time, the title "Dragon" became synonymous with great leadership and courage.

References to dragons first appeared in the *Mabinogi*, a foundational collection of Welsh stories, and have since permeated Welsh history. Kings, leaders, and even heads of state adopted the dragon as an emblem of power and unity. Today, Y Ddraig Goch is one of the most iconic symbols of Wales, representing the nation's mythology, history, and identity. Its image still proudly decorates the Welsh flag today.

VARIATIONS

During the reign of a king named Lludd Llaw, a Red Dragon lived high in the Cambrian Mountains in central Wales. It harmed no one, and the king was happy to live alongside the creature. The country was then invaded by evil dwarves called the Coraniaid from the east. They could hear everything the wind touched across the land, so they grew jealous of the wealth in the west and invaded, using magic against the king's people.

They sent a deadly White Dragon. As the White Dragon approached, all seemed lost—until the wild Red Dragon rose in defense of the land and a deadly battle ensued. The huge beasts spread across the skies, spitting fire at one another and plunging the country into ruin. Women miscarried, the land became barren, and no one slept thanks to the terrible screeching of the mighty dragons.

King Lludd's brother figured out a cunning loophole in the Coraniaid's ability to hear everything. He held up a drinking horn to cover his mouth, whispering into it as his brother held the tip to his ear. The Coronaiad couldn't hear a word. King Lludd and his brother made a plan.

Aloud, King Lludd made a speech to his people, declaring that there was no hope and they must send messages of surrender. The Coraniaid arrived, only to have a poison potion poured over them, destroying them instantly.

There remained the problem of the White Dragon. A huge pit was dug, filled with mead and covered with cloth so the two fighting dragons landed on the pit and fell into it. Both of them drank deeply after years of fighting. The mead intoxicated them, and they fell into a drunken stupor.

The men bound both beasts and dragged them off to a hill in Snowdonia in the northwest of modern-day Wales, buried them in a huge stone chest, and covered it in a lake of water before filling in the rest of the hill.

THE STORY YOU NEED TO KNOW

Long ago, a king named Vortigern (also called Gwrtheyrn) became concerned that the newly arrived Saxons posed a threat to the well-being of his people, the Britons. He invited them to a feast to try and preempt

any violence but was betrayed by his guests and forced to flee to the Snowdonian hills in search of safety. There with his loyal followers, he intended to build a fortress on a hill, later called Emrys' Hill, in the heart of what is now Wales, to unify the surrounding lands.

The king's men laid the foundations on the top of the hill, but all of the stones would sink into the earth every three days. This happened three times, to the king's dismay. He gathered the druids, and the wise men advised their king that he must break the curse on the land. The only way to do this, they figured, was to find a fatherless boy (if any existed), kill him, spread his blood over the stones, and bury his bones beneath them. It seemed a bit drastic, but the king was desperate, so he sent messengers out to search for such a boy, prioritizing ladies of loose morals.

A literally fatherless boy was found and brought before the king. His name was Myrddin Emrys. The boy's father was a spirit and so Emrys had special powers and told the king he knew what the king was planning, and that it was futile. The boy informed the king that below the hill sat a lake, and in that lake was a stone chest (or a tent or pit, depending on the translation), and in this container, there were two sleeping dragons—one White and one Red. They slept for three days and then would wake, rise from their chest, and fight furiously underhill, causing the ground to move and the stones to sink.

Myrddin Emrys told the king's men to dig down and prove his vision was true. So the men dug, the lake was found and drained, and the chest with two sleeping dragons was found. All stood aghast, but the opening of the chest woke the dragons, and they began to snap and claw at one another.

The White Dragon flew high and swooped down on the Red Dragon time and time again, biting and rending flesh until the Red Dragon's blood oozed from between its scales. Everyone thought the Red Dragon would lose, but it stood firm, and as the White Dragon circled again, it rose to meet it. Facing the attacker fiercely, the Red Dragon roared, and the ground trembled. The White Dragon's nerve broke against this unmoving defense, and it fled. The king's men rejoiced. Everyone loves to see the underdog win!

Myrddin Emrys went on to reveal the symbolism of these two dragons. The Red Dragon represented the Britons, and the White Dragon the Saxons. Though all seemed lost and desperate for the Britons in the face of the Saxon onslaught, the spirit of the Red Dragon and their own were undefeatable.

Now You Know

Y Ddraig Goch is a cherished national emblem embodying the unconquerable spirit of Wales. King Arthur of later English lore used the Golden Dragon as his symbol. Later Arthurian legend even conflated the character of Myrddin Emrys with the better-known wise man Merlin.

The story of Myrddin Emrys is actually older than the one that explains how the dragons got under the hill, with the "prequel" story of Lludd Llaw added much later.

The powerful dragon imagery was adopted in the heraldry of the Tudor Dynasty, particularly by Henry VII, who included the Red Dragon as part of his royal insignia after his victory at the Battle of Bosworth in 1485. Today, The Welsh Dragon stands as an enduring symbol of Welsh culture in the Welsh flag, which was first officially adopted in 1959.

PART 4

HEROES & VILLAINS

In Celtic mythology, heroes are often mortals who can transcend the limits of the human world, journeying into the Otherworld, where only the brave dare to venture. These heroes are often bound by personal *geasa* (sacred promises or prohibitions) as they step through the veil to face challenges with an uncertain chance of return.

The lines between the magical world and real world often get blurred in their stories, as the immortal godlike beings interact with these heroes and stir up great commotion. Today's readers still easily empathize and connect with these heroes through their epic emotions and mystical adventures since they portray heightened levels of angst, loss, fear, and fury. As these epic stories play out in the shared landscape of what it means to be human, each archetypal character sheds further light on the human condition.

Celtic heroes embody humanity in all its messiness and are rarely either purely heroic or entirely villainous. Queen Medb, who rules with fierce courage, offers her own daughter as a prize for her warriors to win. Fionn Mac Cumhaill, the hero who leads with compassion, lets jealousy destroy his legacy. King Bran, who united his people, turns to genocide against his rivals. It's up to the storyteller and listener to choose what side, if any, they take in tales of war and conflict; the heroes themselves remain powerful, alluring, and ambiguous.

PWYLL

Pronunciation: POOY-TH
Also Known As: The Prince of Dyfed; Hero of "The First Branch of the Mabinogi"; Friend of the Otherworld

Pwyll, prince of Dyfed, was a ruler, warrior, and hunter, best known for his encounters with Annwn (the Otherworld). Pwyll exemplifies many of the qualities of a Welsh hero: He's handsome, strong, and a little too generous for his own good.

The Story You Need to Know

Pwyll's story begins like many great Celtic adventures: while he was out hunting. He chased after a white female deer, which stayed just out of reach of his pack of hounds and moved into an unfamiliar territory.

Pwyll should probably have realized that he'd crossed over into Annwn, the Otherworld, by the white color of the deer. He should definitely have noticed when a rival pack of hounds brought it down, since they were white with red ears. (If white-colored animals hinted at an Otherworldly origin, white-colored animals with red ears shouted it out loud while waving a big flag.) But Pwyll was fixated on his prize and drove off the hounds to claim the white deer for himself. It was only when the ruler of Annwn himself, Arawn, appeared, enraged at the insult, that Pwyll finally deduced where he was and what was going on.

Arawn set his price for forgiveness: He and Pwyll were to swap lives for a year and a day. He promptly enchanted them to look like one another and headed off for Dyfed to take up Pwyll's duties. Pwyll settled

into his role as the Lord of the Otherworld, aware that at some point he would have to fight Arawn's great rival, Hafgan. His biggest problem at first, however, proved to be putting off the amorous advances of Arawn's wife, who thought he was her husband. Pwyll had no wish to further offend Arawn and had to come up with ever more creative ways to get out of his marital duties.

Near the end of the year, Hafgan attacked, and Pwyll managed to fell him with one blow. By refusing to strike a second time and put the wounded man out of his misery, he thwarted Hafgan's ability to recover from his wounds and defeated him once and for all, which Arawn had never managed to do.

Arawn was pleased with Pwyll for defeating his rival, and even more pleased with him for not sleeping with his wife, and declared Pwyll "friend of the Otherworld" when it came time for them to trade back.

It was possibly due to this friendship that Rhiannon decided to pursue Pwyll. They were engaged for a year and a day, but Pwyll made a terrible mistake on the day of their wedding feast. A beggar asked him for a favor, and Pwyll effusively promised him "anything in my power." The beggar promptly revealed himself to be Gwawl ap Clud, Rhiannon's former fiancé, and he asked for Rhiannon's hand and for the wedding feast. Poor Pwyll could not think of anything to get out of this, but fortunately, Rhiannon figured out a loophole, and thanks to her, the couple were wed after another year's delay.

Their married life went well for several years, but it was complicated by their lack of an heir, which made the nobles of Dyfed uneasy. Pwyll came under pressure to put Rhiannon aside and take another wife, but he loved her too much to do so. To their great joy, she became pregnant at last, but their son, Pryderi, disappeared the same night he was born. Rhiannon was accused of eating him!

Pwyll couldn't bring himself to believe that his wife did that, and he still refused to set her aside. Rhiannon took on a penance for the crime without complaint and still joined Pwyll at the feasting hall every evening.

Eventually, Rhiannon was vindicated when their long-lost son turned up (see Pryderi's entry for his full story), and all was well once more in the kingdom of Dyfed. It turned out that the child had vanished, and Rhiannon's maids had made up the cannibalism story to get out of being blamed.

Pwyll and Rhiannon ruled side by side for many years, until Pwyll's eventual death in the disastrous invasion of Ireland (see the entry on Bran and Branwen for more on that battle).

PRYDERI

PRONUNCIATION: **PRUH-DERRY**
ALSO KNOWN AS: **THE PRINCE OF DYFED; GWRI OF THE GOLDEN HAIR**

Pryderi, prince of Dyfed, is the only character in Welsh myth to turn up in all four branches of the *Mabinogi*, though he is more prominent in some than others. He is the son of Pwyll and Rhiannon, and his Otherworldly blood comes through in his rapid growth from childhood to adolescence, and in his continuing friendship and connection to the Lord of the Otherworld, Arawn.

THE STORY YOU NEED TO KNOW

Pryderi's name means "anxiety," but for the first four years of his life, he was called Gwri of the Golden Hair. He was raised by a lord of Dyfed called Teyrnon. By the time Gwri was four years old, he had the height and maturity of an adolescent, and so Teyrnon sat him down and told him how he had been adopted by the couple.

One night, Teyrnon stayed up to watch over his prize white mare as she was giving birth. For the past two years, she'd given birth to a foal on that same night, but the foal had disappeared without a trace. So Teyrnon was sure something uncanny was going on and decided to wait up.

Sure enough, at midnight, a huge clawed hand reached into the stable to seize the newborn foal. Teyrnon struck it with his sword and cut off the hand, hearing a shriek from overhead. He never saw the creature that the arm belonged to, but when he got a little closer, he saw a baby boy clutched in the severed hand.

As the years went by, Teyrnon and his wife began to notice the strong resemblance between their foster child and Pwyll, the prince of Dyfed. When he heard about this similarity, young Gwri decided to go and find his real parents. He made his way to Pwyll's castle and met a beautiful woman (who turned out to be Rhiannon) sitting on a stump at the castle gates. She told him she had eaten her own son on the night of his birth. Gwri asked her to walk with him and told her his story along the way. When Pwyll came out to meet his guest, the resemblance was striking—it was like a mirrored image, with their age difference the only thing distinguishing the two.

Rhiannon renamed Gwri Pryderi because of all the worry he'd caused her. Pryderi was fostered with another lord of Dyfed, Pendaran Dyfed, until he grew up with every skill and talent and married Cygfa.

Pryderi joined in the invasion of Ireland and was one of the mere seven people who returned from the entire fleet (see Bran and Branwen's entry for this full story). The severed head of Bran the Blessed told the survivors how to live without any wants or needs for eighty years in the Otherworld, but their idyll eventually ended. Pryderi's best friend, Manawydan, would have been next in line for the throne of all what is now Great Britain, but in the intervening years, another king had been chosen, so Manawydan returned to Dyfed with Pryderi.

Either time moved differently in Dyfed, or Rhiannon cast a spell, since she and Pryderi's wife, Cygfa, were still waiting for Pryderi's return and threw a huge feast to welcome him back after those eighty years. At the feast, Pryderi noticed the red-hot chemistry between his best friend and his mother, and he suggested they get married.

The two couples had a few years of blissful rule in Dyfed before a terrible curse blighted the land, shrouding it in mist and removing all living creatures but the four of them. Pryderi and his wife, mother, and best friend/stepfather spent several years wandering through the neighboring lands, trying to make a living as crafters. Unfortunately for them, they were too skilled and kept being driven out of towns by lesser, jealous crafters.

When they finally decided to return to Dyfed, Pryderi was waylaid on a magical boar hunt. Once more showing a distinct resemblance to his father, Pryderi ignored the Otherworldly appearance of the white boar and followed it into an eerie tower, where Pryderi fell under an enchantment. It was only when Manawydan broke the curse that Pryderi was reunited with Cygfa and Dyfed was restored.

Years later, the Lord of the Otherworld, Arawn, gave Pryderi a great gift: the first pigs in Wales. This hitherto unknown animal was widely celebrated as being like a wild boar but much smoother and more docile (and delicious). Arawn warned Pryderi not to give the pigs away.

Gwydion, an entertainer from the neighboring kingdom of Gwynedd to the north, asked for the pigs as a gift for his performance, but Pryderi refused. Gwydion returned with a better offer: He had a herd of horses and a pack of hounds to trade. As a trade wouldn't violate the terms of his agreement with Arawn, Pryderi agreed to swap the pigs for the horses and hounds.

Unbeknownst to him, the sole purpose for Gwydion's visit was to stir up a war between Dyfed and Gwynedd. Gwydion drove the pigs away and told a tall tale in his home court about how he was thrown out in disgrace. The horses and hounds turned to dust. Pryderi had unknowingly broken his promise to Arawn and had to go to war with Gwynedd.

The king of Gwynedd (Math fab Mathonwy) and his armies defeated Pryderi and the warriors of Dyfed three times, at heavy cost. After a pivotal battle, Pryderi agreed to the rite of single combat to prevent more deaths. He fought against the same Gwydion who had started the war and lost because of Gwydion's skill and power at enchantment.

Now You Know

A central character to the *Mabinogi*, and the only character to appear in all four branches, Pryderi is a key figure in Welsh mythology. The Chronicles of Prydain book series by Lloyd Alexander, which is loosely based on Welsh myth, features a character called King Pryderi who appears in the final book of the series.

BRAN & BRANWEN

PRONUNCIATION: **BRAN**; **BRON**-win; **BRAN**-win
ALSO KNOWN AS: BRAN THE BLESSED, BENDIGEIDFRAN
(PRONOUNCED **BEN-I-GED**-vran); BRONWYN

Bran was king of the whole Isle of the Mighty (modern-day Great Britain). He was a giant who relied more on wisdom than strength and was one of three famous children of the imprisoned god Llŷr. His sister Branwen was clever, beautiful, and highly principled, committed to creating a lasting peace.

THE STORY YOU NEED TO KNOW

All the lords and ladies were assembled at Harlech in northern Wales, when the High King of Ireland, Matholwch, arrived with a proposal. He had come in full pomp and circumstance, with his retinue riding on his herd of prize horses, to propose an alliance between the two islands. This had never been achieved before. He asked for Branwen's hand in marriage to seal the alliance.

Bran consulted all of his lords and advisers to see what they thought of the proposal. He also asked Branwen, who was eager for such a peaceful resolution, and his brother Manawydan, who also agreed that this would be a great match. He neglected to consult his half-brothers, Nisien and Efnisien, who shared a mother with the children of Llŷr. Efnisien was so offended by this omission that he decided to sabotage the alliance.

At the wedding feast, Efnisien snuck into the stables and brutally mutilated the Irish horses, cutting and disfiguring them as a deliberate act of disrespect and malice toward the Irish king.

When the crime was discovered, Matholwch was distraught. Bran offered recompense in the form of gold and silver for each horse, but only the gift of a magical cauldron was enough to assuage the crime. This cauldron could bring life back to any dead bodies placed within it.

With these amends paid, Branwen set off for Ireland with her new husband. At first, things went well. As the queen of Ireland, she ruled alongside her husband. They had a son, Gwern, who was duly fostered out to a noble family.

But gradually, word of the mutilation and insult to the king spread and bred discontent. People started to blame and resent Branwen for it. Matholwch did nothing to protect her. Over time, things escalated, starting with small asides and snide comments, progressing to "accidental" blows, and then on to outright violence. Branwen suffered in silence, not wanting to undermine the peace treaty.

She was eventually reduced to the status of a servant, working in the kitchens. Matholwch worried that word of her mistreatment was going to get back to her brother, but rather than address the behavior of his people, he blocked all communications between the islands.

Branwen was resourceful, and with no human allies, she turned to the natural world. She found a baby starling and hand-reared it. She taught it the power of human speech, how to navigate across the ocean, and how to recognize the face of her brother Bran. When the starling was ready, she sent it across the Irish Sea to find her brother and tell him about her plight.

When the starling found Bran and gave him the message, Bran was furious. He was usually a temperate and measured ruler, but in this case, he decided to go to war. Leaving a council of seven wise elders in charge of the kingdom, he called on 154 *cantrefs* (which were provinces or smaller kingdoms) of Great Britain to send their fighting men and assembled an army. This was not to be a war of conquest, but a war of annihilation. Bran intended for every last man, woman, and child in Ireland to die.

The armies assembled from all corners of Great Britain. Bran himself led the fleet, wading across the Irish Sea, with the ships following behind. On those ships were Pwyll, Pryderi, Bran's brother Manawydan, and Efnisien, whose crime had instigated everything.

The Irish were vastly outnumbered but fought fiercely. Whenever they were driven back, the invaders burned the land—crops, fields, and even homes were put to the torch. Branwen heard about the war and realized what her brother was doing. Despite her ill treatment, she had no wish for genocide, so she begged her husband to make peace.

Matholwch and Bran came to terms. Ireland would pay tribute, and Gwern, the child of both royal houses, would rule over both islands when he grew up. They planned to celebrate this new treaty in a feasting hall built specifically for this purpose.

Efnisien suspected treachery and was proved right when his inspection of the hall turned up sacks left at the foot of every pillar. The servants told him that the sacks were full of food, but Efnisien discovered that they held warriors poised for ambush. He squeezed each sack, quietly killing the warriors inside and defusing the Irish trap.

The feast went ahead, and Branwen, who had known nothing of the trap, presented her son Gwern as the heir of both lands. Efnisien called the child to come to him, and when Branwen encouraged young Gwern to go to his uncle, Efnisien declared that he would not allow peace, no matter how high the price, and threw the child into the fire, killing him.

The hall erupted into fighting. This time, the Irish made use of the magical cauldron to bring their dead back to life to rejoin the fray, and the British forces were on the defensive. Efnisien sacrificed his life to destroy the magic cauldron by leaping into it while he was alive. With that powerful magic ended, both sides fought on to near total destruction.

After the smoke cleared, only seven of the invaders were left alive, Branwen among them. They carried Bran's severed head, which retained the power of speech for a time, with them. Branwen died of grief on the way home.

In Ireland, four pregnant women survived, and Welsh tradition has it that their incestuous descendants populated the four provinces of Ireland. Irish tradition disputes this, saying that the provinces were created much earlier than this by the Fir Bolg (as described in *The Book of Invasions*).

Bran's head was able to advise the survivors and direct them to an island paradise, where they lived for eighty years without grief or want. Bran's head is said to have been buried under the hill where the Tower of London stands today, facing France to ward off invasion from that quarter.

Now You Know

Bran the Blessed gives his name to the character of Bran in George R. R. Martin's series A Song of Ice and Fire (*A Game of Thrones* is the first book in the series). The myth shows clearly how one might tell the same tale with a completely different perspective on who is "good" and who is "bad," a kind of gray morality that comes up often in Celtic myths. The Welsh villain Efnisien creates almost all of the conflict in his attempt to block the peace treaty, the wise and kindly Bran embarks on a genocidal war, and the Irish people as a whole persecute the innocent Branwen for a crime she had no part in. There is treachery and bad behavior on all sides, and the ultimate "truth" of where the heroes reside is in the hands of the storyteller.

MANAWYDAN

PRONUNCIATION: MAN-A-WAD-AN

This Welsh hero shares a name (but nothing more) with the Irish deity Manannán Mac Lir. He is the principal character of "The Third Branch of the Mabinogi"—a king in exile who leads his companions in search of a better life, and he ultimately succeeds in renewing their homeland.

The Story You Need to Know

Brother of Bran and Branwen, Manawydan was one of only seven survivors of Bran's ill-fated invasion of Ireland. After returning, Bran's severed head retained its ability to speak, and it steered the survivors to an island paradise where they spent the next eighty years without pain or want. After eighty years, they forgot why they weren't supposed to open a certain door, and by opening it, they broke the spell and ended their sojourn.

Manawydan had been next in line for the throne of the Isle of the Mighty (aka Great Britain) when he'd left with Bran, but after eighty years, the country had moved on and chosen a new king. Fortunately, his best friend Pryderi invited Manawydan to stay in Dyfed with him and his wife, Cygfa, for as long as he needed.

At the homecoming feast, Manawydan found himself enchanted with his best friend's mother, Rhiannon. The conversation flowed all night. She was intelligent, generous, charming, and witty. He was contemplating how to broach this delicate subject with Pryderi the next day, but Pryderi put him out of his misery and actually suggested that

Manawydan and Rhiannon get married! This solidified Manawydan's already high opinion of his friend.

After the wedding, all was well in Dyfed for a time. Then one night, disaster struck. A magical mist descended on the land, taking every living creature with it except for Manawydan, Rhiannon, Pryderi, and Cygfa. Not an insect stirred. The four had to leave, as nothing could survive on this blighted land.

They spent the next year wandering around Britain, trying to make a living as crafters. Unfortunately, they were just too talented. They were able to make better goods than any ordinary people and knew how to dye them blue, which was beyond the skill of any crafters in those days. They were driven out of every town they tried to settle in, until all of the crafters joined together to drive them out of the country entirely.

They then decided to return to Dyfed and try to eke out a living. On their way back, Pryderi followed a white boar into a mysterious tower and never returned. Manawydan's wife Rhiannon was furious that he'd left Pryderi alone and insisted on following him, but she also failed to return, and the tower vanished in the night.

Feeling a little unhinged by all these losses, Manawydan and Cygfa tried again to make it work as crafters in England and were once again pushed out. They made their way back to Dyfed and planted three fields of wheat in a last-ditch attempt to live on the cursed land. The wheat grew, but just before they were due to harvest the first field, all of the wheat vanished in the night; the same happened with the second field.

Manawydan stood vigil over the third field of wheat, their last food and final hope for survival. In the night, hundreds of mice—the first living things he'd seen in Dyfed in years—emerged and began to eat the wheat.

Acting fast, Manawydan grabbed one of the mice and put it in his glove. He was not able to save the wheat, but he showed the mouse to

Cygfa and declared his intention: to hang the mouse as a thief, and a warning to all other mouse-thieves! Cygfa wasn't sure how this mouse-based vendetta was going to help with their imminent starvation, but she left him to it.

Manawydan went alone to a hilltop to construct a teeny tiny gibbet (a hanging structure) with a teeny tiny noose so that his mouse execution could proceed.

As he was engaged in this macabre (yet strangely adorable) crafting project, a scholar, a priest, and a bishop approached him in turn, each pleading for the mouse's life, offering successively greater payments in exchange for her release. Manawydan turned them all down. Finally, the bishop asked Manawydan what it would take for him to let the mouse go.

Whether he expected to receive it or not, Manawydan laid out everything he wanted in return: He wanted Pryderi and Rhiannon back, he wanted the mist gone, he wanted the people of Dyfed and all the animals and creatures that lived there to be returned safe and unharmed.

Surprisingly, his wish was granted! The bishop revealed his true identity. He was Llwyd ap Cil Coed, the same Otherworldly sorcerer who had cursed Dyfed in the first place as a favor to his old friend Gwawl ap Clud, who was still not over Rhiannon, and who had made the magical tower that captured Pryderi and Rhiannon. When Cygfa and Manawydan planted their wheat, he'd turned all of his household into mice to eat the wheat and drive them off again. He'd come to Manawydan twice before, disguised as a scholar and a priest. And the mouse that Manawydan was holding in custody in his glove was the sorcerer's own wife.

Manawydan got his best friend, his home, and his wife back as the curse was lifted from Dyfed and the skies were seen for the first time in years. The foursome settled down to rule Dyfed well and wisely for many more years.

Now You Know

Unlike the Irish god whose name he shares, Manawydan fab Llŷr firmly lives in the realm of the hero, interacting with the Otherworld without being part of it. His determination to punish the only creature he could was ultimately rewarded when it led to the enchantment being broken.

CULHWCH & OLWEN

Pronunciation: CUL-wich; OL-wen
Also Known As: Kulhwch, Kilhwch

Culhwch's quest for the giant's daughter Olwen is a classic in Celtic mythology. Given a list of seemingly impossible tasks, the irrepressibly optimistic Culhwch never wavers in his determination to win the hand of a woman he has never met. As he is aided by his famous cousin King Arthur, this is also the oldest recorded Arthurian tale.

The Story You Need to Know

Culhwch's family history was complicated. His mother went mad while she was pregnant and gave birth to him in a pigsty before regaining her sanity and promptly dying. His father decided that he needed a new wife and decided to murder a neighboring king and steal his queen. Understandably, the queen never forgave her new husband.

When Culhwch returned from his foster family as a young man, his stepmother, the queen, told him that he could only marry Olwen, the beautiful daughter of the terrible giant Ysbaddaden. This seemed to function as a magical spell, because as soon as he heard Olwen's name, Culhwch fell in love with her completely and was determined to win her hand.

Culhwch's father advised him to go to his cousin King Arthur for help, and Culhwch set out. He was initially refused entry to Arthur's hall because the feast had already started. In a scene reminiscent of Lugh's entry to Tara (see Lugh Lamhfada's entry for that story), he had to debate with the gatekeeper to be allowed in. He proved his worth to Arthur by reciting the names and talents of every single hero in attendance in the hall. Some of the names might be familiar to a reader of the Knights of the Round Table today, but many others are found only in this story, hinting at an even earlier oral tradition that did not survive.

Arthur hand-picked a small group to go with Culhwch to seek out the giant's castle, and they made their way there. It turned out that Culhwch's maternal aunt was married to the giant's brother and lived on his land. She told Culhwch that she had to keep her youngest son locked up in a chest, because Ysbaddaden had murdered every one of her children that he'd found. He killed all visitors, especially young men. He only allowed craftsmen with a useful skill to enter his castle.

One of Arthur's men, Cai (see his story in Cath Palug's entry), offered to go and polish the giant's sword. Whether that struck the medieval Welsh as an innuendo—or whether they felt that the extended sword-polishing scene that followed was perfectly tame—is a question for the academics. Having gained entry, and taken hold of the giant's "sword," Cai threatened Ysbaddaden and demanded that he let Culhwch in.

The giant revealed why he was so prone to killing any young men within reach: The day of his daughter's wedding would be the day of his death. But now that he had been asked, he laid out the tasks that would need to be completed before a wedding could take place. Ever optimistic, Culhwch accepted each impossible task that Ysbaddaden named. But every time he accepted a task, Ysbaddaden responded that he couldn't complete it without first completing a different task…And this went on for over forty tasks.

The tasks boiled down to two main quests: to plant, plow, and harvest a particular field nearby that had been barren for years so that they would have food for the feast; and to get the razor, scissors, and comb from between the ears of the terrible wild boar, the Twrch Trwyth, so that the giant could have a shave and a haircut on the wedding morning. (You read that correctly.) The rest of the tasks were the things Culhwch would need to do in order to complete those main tasks, or marvels that the giant wanted him to gather, at great risk to life and limb.

Making the barren field produce corn proved relatively easy: One of Arthur's men, Gwrhyr, spoke every language in the world, including the languages of animals, and he asked the local ants for help. With the natural world on his side, the barren field was made to produce wheat for the wedding feast.

The bulk of the tasks formed the tale of the hunt for the Twrch Trwyth. Hunters, horses, weapons, and hounds had to be gathered. Arthur himself led an army across the sea to Ireland, where the Twrch Trwyth was rampaging. The Irish thought they were being invaded and resisted King Arthur for a while until everyone figured out what was going on. The hunting party discovered that this boar was once an evil king, who had been transformed into a boar because of his wickedness (which sort of explained why he had a shaving kit in between his ears, and sort of…didn't).

After killing the boar (see King Arthur's entry) and gathering the last of the marvels (the blood of a hellish hag), Arthur's men descended on the giant's castle. Extremely annoyed by all the trouble they had to go through, they shaved him to the bone using the deadly sharp razor they'd obtained from the boar, shaving off first hair, then skin, and finally flesh. They cut off the giant's head and mounted it outside the castle.

Culhwch married Olwen, who was so lovely that little flowers grew in her footsteps, and the two remained married until the end of their days, which at least suggests that they were happier together than Culhwch's father and his second wife.

Now You Know

While Culhwch has not made his way into modern adaptations, his tale is considered the prototype for a type of story called "The Giant's Daughter" which is quintessentially Celtic. In it, a reluctant father sends a would-be bridegroom on a series of seemingly impossible quests, only to have the bridegroom succeed and the wedding go ahead, often causing the reluctant father's death. There are many other versions of this tale, including *The King of Ireland's Son*, a 1916 children's novel by Padraic Colum.

KING ARTHUR

PRONUNCIATION: AR-thur
ALSO KNOWN AS: THE ONCE AND FUTURE KING, ARTHUR PENDRAGON

King Arthur needs no introduction. After all, the legendary king who united England against the Saxon invaders—and straddled the line between pagan and Christian—has been the subject of numerous films, books, and reinterpretations.

In Welsh mythology, an older version of Arthur predates the better known. The earliest text, written by a Welsh monk, depicts Arthur not as a king but as a brave warrior and a great leader of men who fought fiercely against the Saxons and won many battles. This image serves as the stepping stone for the Arthur we know today—an ideal king whose wisdom and good judgment elevated his leadership, allowing him to preside over a court of extraordinary heroes.

VARIATIONS

Some of the kings of Celtic mythology butt up against a fuzzy line between historic fact and mythological invention. At times, great stories have been created to heighten the significance of actual rulers. Similar to Arthur, the semi-historical Irish king Cormac Mac Airt's story became a unifying myth for Ireland, as he was said to have codified the Brehon Law, a legal code in Ireland based on restorative justice through the clan system, which has never been repealed. He won his throne by passing wise judgment rather than fighting his way to the throne.

An example of this restorative justice can be seen in the story of a poor old woman, whose sheep had gotten into a queen's garden and eaten her flowers; the then-king pronounced that her sheep should be confiscated and given to the queen, leaving the woman destitute. Cormac objected and declared that the queen's flowers would grow back, like the wool of a sheep, and so it should be "a shearing for a shearing," giving the queen that year's fleece. The judgment was so wise that he was declared the new king then and there. During Cormac's harmonious reign, it was said that the woods were full of game, the rivers full of fish, crops produced three times more than what they normally did, and every neighbor's voice was sweet to the ear.

THE STORY YOU NEED TO KNOW

The oldest version of King Arthur appears in the story of Culhwch and Olwen as an already famous and powerful leader. Culhwch's first stop on his adventure to win the hand of Olwen, the giant's daughter, was to go to King Arthur and ask for his help, as he would otherwise be doomed to failure. Arthur's hall had its established traditions; no one was allowed to enter once the feasting had started, because one of the main duties of the Celtic king was to host a feast and ensure that all of his allies were rewarded and honored by his generosity.

As Culhwch's quest, with its many nested tasks, unfolded, Arthur showed his discernment and skill in picking the right person for each task: sending his knights Cai and Gawain with Culhwch to find the giant, assigning the hero Gwrhyr Gwalstawt Ieithoedd, who could speak every language, to act as their guide, and continually choosing the right man for the job as the tasks went on. The most important, risky, and protracted of the tasks was to kill the Twrch Trwyth, a cursed boar that was terrorizing Ireland. Culhwch was tasked with defeating this boar to

retrieve a comb, scissors, and a razor that it kept between its ears, for reasons best known to the boar.

The day came that all of the heroes were assembled along with their magical weapons, and King Arthur himself led them across the sea to Ireland to hunt the terrible boar and its terrible boar-children. Unfortunately, he did not think to give the locals a heads-up, and the group was met with fierce opposition by Irish warriors, who thought (not unreasonably) that they were being invaded.

When at last everything was cleared up, and all of the humans were united against all of the boars, Arthur found out that the boar was an evil king who had been cursed to take the form of a boar along with all four of his wicked children, possibly because they all refused to have any vowels in their names. That piece of information didn't necessarily help them defeat the boar, but the fact that the boars were all transformed humans did explain why he wouldn't fall for any hunters' tricks and seemed preternaturally intelligent.

The combined forces of all of the hunters together managed to kill one of the boar's children, and the Twrch Trwyth and his remaining boar-sons swam back across the Irish Sea to rampage across Wales and England. King Arthur and his army were in hot pursuit. With the help of Mabon ap Modron (see the entry about Aengus Óg), Gwyn ap Nudd (see the entry about Arawn), and Manawydan fab Llŷr, the terrible boar was finally driven into the sea, with the comb, scissors, and razor that Culhwch needed for Olwen's father snatched from between his ears on the way.

Now You Know

The King Arthur of medieval literature shares many characteristics with the original warrior of Welsh mythology, with the addition of a magic sword, a wizard, and a round table for all of his extraordinary followers to sit around. The Welsh Arthur fought against Saxon invaders and became a unifying myth for Britain and, later, a literary character of note. Adaptations abound in popular culture, from the 1963 Disney animation *The Sword in the Stone* to the 1981 classic film *Excalibur* to the 2021 film *The Green Knight*. Literary adaptations date as far back as the Middle Ages, with the French poet Chrétien de Troyes codifying many of the aspects familiar to readers today and inventing an early form of the novel along the way.

NESSA

Pronunciation: **NESS**-uh, **NYA**-sa
Also Known As: Assa (pronounced **AY**-sa), Easa the Gentle, Nessa the Ungentle

Nessa is a background figure in the Ulster Cycle and is mostly featured as a mentor and guide to her son, the young Conchobar Mac Nessa. She is a force to be reckoned with, but later fades from the narrative. Her origin story deserves to be better known.

Though her tale starts off in privilege, after witnessing the brutal murder of her entire family, she goes on to embody female rage and bloody vengeance like few before or after her. Her ability to survive, endure great hardship, and pursue her goals single-mindedly earned her the name "Ungentle."

The Story You Need to Know

Nessa grew up as the daughter of a powerful chieftain in Ulster. In those days, she was called Assa, which means "The Gentle One." She loved learning above all else, and her indulgent father hired thirteen tutors to answer all her questions and teach her everything she wanted to know.

Everything changed in one terrible night, when raiders attacked and killed everyone in the house. Only Assa escaped by hiding under the bed, hearing the death cries of her family. She then had to learn to survive in the wilderness alone, living off her considerable wits and devoting herself to arts of the warrior.

Before long, Assa had reinvented herself. She vowed vengeance on the raiders who had destroyed her home and family and commenced a quest to hunt them all down and murder them whenever she found one, swiftly moving on to her next target without remorse. During this time, she amassed a following of fellow warriors. The name Assa no longer fit, so she began to be called Ní-assa, shortened to Nessa: The Ungentle One. Rumor of her quest got out, and those who were on her list lived in fear until they met their bloody end at her hand.

Eventually, Nessa's quest for vengeance came to an end. She reconciled with the last of the raiders, who had left behind his murderous ways to become a druid. Now called Cathbad, he would later be an important adviser to her son and future king, Conchobar. Cathbad convinced Nessa to spare his life by offering her a prophecy: Any child conceived on that day would become a great king. Nessa's ambition for her future children outweighed her need for vengeance, so she and Cathbad conceived a child together. Cathbad's role as the father of her children was not considered particularly important, and so her son was named after her: Conchobar Mac Nessa. This was common in ancient Ireland, where surnames were often matrilineal.

When she went into labor with her son, Cathbad told Nessa that the *following* day, December 25, would be a more auspicious time to birth a son who would be king. This date was likely added later to link Conchobar more strongly to Christian tradition. So, showcasing her stubbornness, her powerful dedication, and an extreme tolerance for pain, Nessa sat herself on top of a rock and held in the baby, extending her labor until the following day. After being under such immense pressure, the baby popped out like a cork and landed in the River Conchobar—and that's how he got his name.

Nessa arrived in Emain Macha, the seat of the Ulster kings, as a woman with a history. She had won fame and renown as a warrior, had a son in tow, and was still unmarried. The king of Ulster, Fergus Mac Róich, was smitten and asked for her hand in marriage. Nessa named a rather outrageous bride price: She wanted her son to rule Ulster as king for the next year. Through political maneuvering, advising her son every step of the way, Nessa managed to parlay this temporary kingskip into permanent rule for Conchobar.

SCATHACH

PRONUNCIATION: SKA-HAWK
ALSO KNOWN AS: DAUGHTER OF THE MORRÍGAN, THE SHADOWY ONE

Not much survives from the story of this great Scottish warrior queen. Like her name, which means "The Shadowy One," she has faded into obscurity. It is likely only her connection with the Irish hero Cúchulainn that preserves her memory, but there is speculation that Scathach was once at the center of her own epic story. This story was not written down and transmitted, which, sadly, is all too common when it comes to women who did not fit within the role that later society wished to impose on them. Our ancient world was, perhaps, more free than we dare to dream.

THE STORY YOU NEED TO KNOW

After her career as a great warrior, its story now lost, Scathach had won enough renown to establish a training school for warriors on an island off Scotland. To get there, prospective warriors had to traverse the wilderness of the Scottish Highlands and cross a magical bridge of her construction that connected the island to the mainland. The bridge first appeared to be a suspension bridge with a thorny rope that could not be gripped for balance, but as soon as a warrior stepped foot on the bridge, it would narrow and twist and attempt to throw the warrior off, as if the bridge were a living thing.

After passing this entrance test, Scathach would put the prospective student in one particular house and set all her current pupils against the

aspirant. Only if they overcame those tests would she agree to train the warrior.

A great deal of Celtic warfare revolved around a rite called single combat, and a large part of single combats were feats. Typically, two sides in a battle would each nominate a champion, and those two warriors would square off. Before fighting, each would have a chance to perform a series of feats: displays of physical and athletic prowess designed to intimidate their opponent. One combatant might concede the match at this point, avoiding bloodshed altogether, and this was considered a good outcome. Many feats only survive in evocative names, like the apple feat, the salmon leap, or the thunder strike. Others are described more fully, such as the shield feat, in which a warrior would set their shield spinning and balance their full body weight on the edge while it continued to spin.

Scathach specialized in seemingly impossible feats. She taught a spear feat that involved standing a spear upright in the ground, salmon leaping above it, and coming to land with the sternum against the speartip, without breaking the skin.

Scathach offered the gift of prophecy to some of her pupils, drawing back the veil to look into their futures for them. She famously crafted a terrible spear called the Gae Bulga from the bones of sea monsters who had killed one another and washed up on shore. This terrible spear carried the violence of its creation, magically seeking out the weakest point on the body to penetrate. Once it had pierced the skin, the spearhead splintered into hundreds of barbs, piercing one's organs. It was so thoroughly devastating that it could not be pulled out through the entry wound but had to be pushed through the body of its unfortunate victim, pulling their entrails with it. Wielding this spear was a feat in itself, as it had to be held between the toes and thrown from under the water to find its mark.

Her best pupil was another Scottish warrior called Aoife, but after a time the two women became rivals, and Aoife raided Scathach frequently, providing practice for the latter's trainees.

Scathach's story survives in large part due to her link with the Irish warrior Cúchulainn. He sought her out for training. Unbeknownst to him, this was a mere ploy designed to get him away from a scheming nobleman's daughter in hopes that he would not survive Scathach's harsh regimen. He did more than survive, thanks in part to the help of his lover, Scathach's daughter Uathach, who is sometimes conflated with the warrior Aoife.

While Cúchulainn was training with Scathach, Aoife attacked. Scathach thought that Cúchulainn was not up to fighting Aoife, knowing their respective skills, and drugged Cúchulainn to keep him safe. He shrugged off the effects of the drug, tricked Aoife into breaking concentration at a crucial moment, and defeated her. The two became lovers after this fight, leading to an apparent reconciliation between Scathach and Aoife.

Before Cúchulainn left, Scathach gave him her prophecy: that he would live a short life, filled with pain, but that his name would be on the lips of storytellers until the end of life and time. She also gave him the Gae Bulga, the spear with which he would later kill his best friend and his own son (see Connla's entry for that tale).

Now You Know

"The Shadowy One" can also be interpreted for how Scathach was overshadowed by later students, with only tantalizing hints remaining of her earlier adventures. The island where she trained warriors is known today as Skye, in the beautiful northwest of Scotland. Since the Mesolithic period, this island has seen various inhabitants—the Celtic tribes, the Picts and the Gaels, and Scandinavian Vikings, to name a few. Plus, for those looking into ancestral connections, two of the most notable and powerful Norse-Gael clans of MacLeod and MacDonald dwelt there. You can still visit Scathach's island and her fortress, known as Dún Scáith (the Fortress of Shadows), which is said to be where she taught her students.

CÚCHULAINN

PRONUNCIATION: KOO-KUL-IN

ALSO KNOWN AS: THE HOUND OF ULSTER, THE HOUND OF CULANN, SETANTA (CHILDHOOD NAME)

Perhaps the best-known Irish mythic hero, Cúchulainn has all the hallmarks you'd expect: semi-divine birth, youthful talent, devastatingly good looks, and a disastrous personal life.

In older stories, his appearance was truly wild: three colors on his hair (black at the root, red in the middle, blond at the tips), seven pupils in each eye, and seven fingers on each hand. In more recent retellings, the supernatural aspects are toned down, his size bulked up to fit an archetypal "hero," and he is often portrayed as much older than he was in the older stories. But by all accounts he was the most beautiful man in Ireland and was described as slender, short, and sad-eyed.

THE STORY YOU NEED TO KNOW

Cúchulainn was Ulster's greatest, yet tragic, champion. He was born in the Otherworld (see Deichtre's entry for that story) and originally called Setanta. He was raised in Ulster and fostered by multiple parents, who taught him a host of skills.

Joining the Boys-Troop of Emain Macha (an early version of a school that was set up by the king of Ulster to train young warriors) at a young age, he fought for acceptance immediately. His brilliance and determination singled him out, isolating him from peers. He won the name Cúchulainn by defeating the monstrous guard dog of the

blacksmith Culann. When the boy witnessed Culann's devastation at the loss of the ferocious dog who had protected him and his lands from all surrounding threats from wolves, bandits, and the Otherworld—while only showing loyalty and affection to Culann—he was remorseful and offered to take the incredible hound's place for a year, until it could be replaced, thereby earning the name Cúchulainn (literally, "Culann's hound").

Ulster's druid Cathbad gave the Boys-Troop a prophecy: Anyone taking up arms for the first time on that day would live a brief, tragic life, but their name would "be on the lips of storytellers until the end of life and time." Cúchulainn alone took the deal. He displayed his famous battle rage for the first time, transforming into a monstrous form. His knees twisted backward like the knees of a hound, his fingernails became claws, his teeth became fangs, a fountain of blood erupted from the top of his head, and one eye bulged to the size of a plate while the other shrank into his skull.

Training in Scotland with Scathach, Cúchulainn won a magical spear (called the Gae Bulga), which eviscerated his opponents. He fathered a child with a Scottish warrior (see Connla's entry to learn more), won magical horses named Liath Macha and Dubh Sainglenn, befriended the Connaught warrior Ferdiad, and married Emer, the only woman in Ireland who was his equal. Cúchulainn was always accompanied by his charioteer, Láeg.

He rejected the advances of the goddess the Morrígan, and hell hath no fury like a woman rejected, so she promised to be the "guardian of his death." Friction persisted between Cúchulainn and the other warriors of Ulster, who were vexed by his three flaws—he was too young (and surpassed warriors twice his age who had worked far harder and longer to get the status they had achieved), too daring (he was brave to the point of stupidity), and too beautiful (everyone was sick of their wives blushing as he walked by). His arrogance could have been a fourth, though this was not seen as a drawback. Needless to say, he wasn't very popular in his time with all the other egomaniacs vying for status.

During the epic *Táin Bó Cúailnge* (when Queen Medb of Connaught invaded Ulster with an army from the south of Ireland), Cúchulainn was Ulster's sole defender, due to the curse of Macha (see the Rhiannon & Macha entry in Part 2 for this story). He managed to delay the march of Medb's army by harrying the army with slingshots and terror tactics. He was able to negotiate the rite of single combat, facing one warrior each morning at the River Dee's shallowest crossing. He comfortably defeated each challenger until the woman-king of Connaught, Medb, convinced Cúchulainn's best friend and fellow student of Scathach, Ferdiad, to fight him. Caught between love and duty, the pair fought a protracted duel over four days. Finally, wounded to the point of death himself, Cúchulainn unleashed his magical spear against Ferdiad, killing him. Wounded and slipping into unconsciousness, he cradled Ferdiad's body, singing a lament: "All was play, all was sport, till came Ferdiad to the ford!"

While Cúchulainn was recovering from the fight with Ferdiad, the army marched unchallenged across Ulster until Cúchulainn's immortal father, Lugh, summoned the only help available: the Boys-Troop. The child-soldiers of Ulster fought bravely, but Cúchulainn awoke to the news that they had all been slaughtered—a generation lost to war. His savage vengeance against the army is a brutal depiction of the devastation of warfare, eventually leaving Cúchulainn wounded and broken-hearted.

Fulfilling his childhood prophecy, Cúchulainn led a brief life. It came to an end when Medb gathered a new army, formed from the families of all the people Cúchulainn had killed in battle, and invaded Ulster again. Cúchulainn was now the official champion of Ulster (see Conall Cearnach's entry), but there was a prophecy that if Ulster's champion died in battle, Ulster would be luckless forever. The people of Ulster tried to hide the invasion from Cúchulainn, but they weren't successful for long. Repeated omens (the entry about Banshees, Bean Nighes, and Cyhyraeths explains these) forewarned that he was heading to his death, but he accepted his fate and carried on.

Another prophecy had been made stating that Cúchulainn's first three spears would kill three kings, and so a small group came to meet Cúchulainn on the way to the fight. The triplet sons of the sorcerer Calatin, who were sorcerers themselves, tried persuading him to hand over the spears, but he threw them in anger, killing each of the sorcerer's sons in turn. The warrior Lugaid Mac Con Roi (avenging Cúchulainn's killing of his father, Cú Roi Mac Dáire) picked up the three spears and threw them back one by one—and one by one they hit three "kings": Liath Macha, king of horses; Cúchulainn's charioteer, Láeg, king of chariot drivers; and Cúchulainn, king of champions.

Stubborn to the end, the mortally wounded Cúchulainn dragged himself to a standing stone (called Clochafarmore, or the Big Man's Stone, which can still be seen in County Louth, in northeast Ireland). Cúchulainn tied himself upright with his own innards, holding his sword aloft. The Morrígan, in the form of a raven, landed on the standing stone and spread her wings over Cúchulainn's body as the young hero died, fulfilling the first half of Cathbad's prophecy.

Cúchulainn's name continues to be on the lips of storytellers, and though we haven't come to the end of time just yet, the second part of that prophecy is still going strong.

Now You Know

Cúchulainn has appeared in pop culture multiple times. His name is mentioned in song, including the title theme of the film *The Boondock Saints*, Thin Lizzy's "Róisín Dubh," and The Pogues' "The Sick Bed of Cúchulainn." He appears in Marvel Comics as part of the Celtic pantheon and is featured in several more comic series, including the Irish-language comic series Cú (also available in English, titled Hound) by Paul Bolger and Barry Devlin. He can also be found in the television show *Gargoyles* and the anime series Fate. A frequent figure in video games, Cúchulainn appears as a character in *SMITE*, as a summonable spirit in *Final Fantasy XII*, and as a demon in *Final Fantasy Tactics* and the Megami Tensei series.

DEICHTRE

PRONUNCIATION: DECK-TRAH
ALSO KNOWN AS: DEICHTINE, DEICHTIRE, THE KING'S CHARIOTEER

Deichtre is the daughter of the druid Cathbad and a woman named Maga, daughter of Aengus Óg. This made her the sister of the king of Ulster, Conchobar Mac Nessa (the Celts often did not distinguish between full and half-siblings, which is one of the reasons the genealogies can get confusing).

As a young woman, she was her brother's charioteer. The charioteer role is an important one in the Ulster Cycle: Charioteers were not warriors themselves, but they drove their warriors into battle. Celtic chariots were drawn by two horses, with room for only one person inside the two-wheeled vehicle. Charioteers stood outside the basket of the chariot, on a piece of wood in between the two horses, where they controlled both animals by the reins, trusting that their warrior would protect them from the battle raging all around. Though descriptions of her revolve around motherhood in most of the stories, her role as the King's Charioteer clearly shows her to have a fearless attitude and an undeniable thirst for adventure.

THE STORY YOU NEED TO KNOW

Deichtre was getting ready for her wedding feast. It was an arranged marriage to an Ulster lord named Súaltam Mac Róich. Though not a forced marriage, she was unenthusiastically preparing for married life with Súaltam. There was nothing objectionable in the match or the man, but her fifty handmaidens were having a hard time coaxing any enthusiasm out of the bride-to-be.

Deichtre saw by a strange trick of the light that the Otherworld was suddenly close at hand, and the veil between the worlds had grown thin, perhaps in response to her longing for something unnamed. On a whim, she called on her Tuatha Dé Danann blood and stepped through to the Otherworld, taking her fifty handmaidens with her.

Their sojourn in the Otherworld was prolonged when Deichtre met a man of the Tuatha Dé Danann—the most beautiful man she had ever seen. He offered her a drink of wine and she moved in with him for the rest of the year.

Over the course of the year in the Otherworld, Deichtre became pregnant. She learned that her lover's name was Lugh. She also realized that she didn't want to stay in the Otherworld forever. Despite all its strange beauty, she missed her home. And, she wanted her child to grow up in Ulster, shaped by its stony soil, deep forests, and familiar people. Deichtre was determined to bring her child home.

But leaving the Otherworld was seldom as simple as entering it, especially after so much time had passed. Deichtre found that she *could* cross back over, but only in the form of a bird. To get her brother's attention, she transformed herself and her fifty handmaidens into a flock of giant birds and crossed the veil. As they swept through the fields, the birds tore up all the spring seedlings, destroying the crops. Furious at the devastation, and sensing something Otherworldly was afoot, the warriors of the Red Branch, Ulster's fighting force, began hunting the flock, unaware of their true identities.

Deichtre led the Red Branch warriors across the borders between worlds and into the Otherworld, where they stumbled across the home she shared with Lugh, each seeing in it a reflection of their own expectations (the dour warrior Bricriu saw a mean hovel; the optimistic champion Fergus saw an opulent palace). Just as Lugh was welcoming them in, Deichtre felt herself struck down with the pains of childbirth. She labored through the night as the warriors slept, and either their sleep or Lugh himself carried her and her handmaidens back through the veil. When the bewildered Ulster warriors awoke the next day on the bare hillside, Deichtre was curled up around her newborn son in the place most familiar to her: her brother's chariot.

Multiple people from Ulster offered to foster her son, embedding him into the community from the start. She named him Setanta (though he was later called Cúchulainn) and put aside her adventurous ways to settle down with her original suitor, Súaltam, in Dún Dealgan (or Dundalk in County Louth in the northeast of Ireland), where they raised Setanta together.

Now You Know

Cúchulainn's supernatural father is often credited for his extraordinary abilities, but his lineage on his mother's side is equally impressive, as she is linked to the Celtic god Aengus Óg. Deichtre was a formidable chariot driver and adventure seeker long before she had the child who would become world-famous.

CONNLA

PRONUNCIATION: CON-la, CON-le
Also Known As: Conlaoch, Son of Aoife

The only son of Cúchulainn and the Scottish warrior woman Aoife, Connla had all the potential to be one of the greatest warriors of all time. But despite his immaculate pedigree, Connla's short life was doomed to tragedy from the very beginning. This is a brutally disastrous story about the needless death of a young man, and it never gets easier to read. Irish mythology seems to revel in this kind of terrible tale.

The Story You Need to Know

When Cúchulainn trained with Scathach, he spent some time as a warrior in her service. One of her most entrenched enemies was her former pupil Aoife. Although Scathach tried to keep Cúchulainn out of the fighting, fearing that he was not good enough to battle Aoife, Cúchulainn distracted Aoife at a crucial moment and got the upper hand against her.

After the battle, the pair became lovers, staying together until Cúchulainn left to return to Ireland. Cúchulainn knew that Aoife was pregnant when he left, and he knew that he was not going to be there to raise his son. He tried to leave his unborn child with a code of conduct that would serve a warrior like himself. He left a ring for the child, and instructions that he be sent to Ireland as soon as he was old enough to wear it on his thumb. And he left three *geasa* (prophecies or taboos; the singular is *geis*).

As a result, Connla was bound to live his life by these three *geasa* or face death if he broke even one. The first: He must never "give up" his name. The second: He must never refuse a challenge to fight. The third: He must never surrender once a fight had begun. We can only assume that Cúchulainn's motive was to ensure his son would follow in his own footsteps and become a great warrior (or die trying).

The first *geis*, to never "give up" his name, can be interpreted in two ways. One reading is that Connla was forbidden from announcing his name first when meeting someone, as doing so was a sign of deference in Cúchulainn's culture. Declaring one's name first ceded status to the other person, and this *geis* ensured Connla would always assert his dominance in social interactions. Alternatively, and slightly more tragically, it can also be understood this *geis* meant Connla could not "give up" or exchange his birth name for another, as Cúchulainn, the once Setanta, had done earlier in his life.

Regardless, Connla grew up on the Isle of Skye with a reconciled Scathach and Aoife—two of the greatest warriors in the world—as mentors and mothers. He took after both of his parents, becoming a formidable fighter at a young age. He was raised with his father's *geasa* as core values and heard only stories of his father's great deeds—shoes he could never fill—and the tale of his father's magic spear, the Gae Bulga. When he was old enough to wear the thumb ring, he set sail for Ireland, alone, to find his father.

And that is, unsurprisingly, where things began to go disastrously wrong.

The court of Emain Macha (the fortress of the king of Ulster and base of the Red Branch warriors) had gathered for a celebration on the coast the day that Connla arrived. When he met the king of Ulster and refused to give his name, the people of Ulster took this as a deep insult. The youth was told that if he did not give his name, he'd have to fight the most prominent warrior there, Conall Cearnach. Of course, Connla accepted the challenge and, to everyone's surprise, roundly defeated Conall Cearnach.

It was at this point that Cúchulainn was sent for, as he was undeniably the greatest warrior in Ulster. Cúchulainn and Connla did not yet know they were father and son. Neither of them wanted to fight, but the youth's stubbornness had made this into a point of honor—the king could not lose face in front of all of his followers by giving this young man his name first.

To his surprise, Cúchulainn found himself in as hard a fight as he'd ever had. After years of winning battles with ease, this one lasted three days and three nights. At last, reluctantly, Cúchulainn called for the Gae Bulga. Connla recognized the name and realized he must be fighting his own father—but his third *geis* stopped him from calling a halt to the fight. Instead, he held up his hand, showing the thumb ring to Cúchulainn.

And Cúchulainn saw it, an instant too late.

The Gae Bulga never missed its target. As Connla lay dying on the strand a moment later, his devastated father sank to his knees and wept.

Cúchulainn's battle rage came over him, and he destroyed the Gae Bulga. The Ulster druid, Cathbad, was so fearful that Cúchulainn would turn on his own people that he put a spell over him. He convinced Cúchulainn that the waves of the ocean were an invading army, and that it was that army that was responsible for Connla's death. And so, Cúchulainn battled the waves for three days more, until he collapsed in heartbroken exhaustion.

Now You Know

W.B. Yeats's play "On Baile's Strand" retells this episode as a dramatic tragedy. The theme of honor and duty coming into conflict with love and relationship is one that is threaded throughout the story of the *Táin* in a complex interplay. Connla's mother, Aoife, is often vilified in retellings of this story, as a clear antagonist is just more satisfying. But there is no "bad guy" in this story. It's a tragic tale where a mother and a father lose their only child. No one wins, everyone loses, and no good or bad guy can be thanked or blamed. Such is the delicacy of Celtic mythology.

CONALL CEARNACH

Pronunciation: **KONE-**al **KYAR-**nak
Also Known As: **The Victorious One**

Conall Cearnach is one of the most formidable, vicious, and terrifying warriors in the Red Branch of Ulster. His appetite for dealing out the death of his enemies was insatiable, and it was said that he did not sleep without the freshly severed head of a Connaught warrior under his knee. Today, we'd call him a psychopath. In those days, warriors held a deeply respected position in Celtic society, making toxic traits quite desirable.

If he had lived at any other time in Ulster, Conall Cearnach would have been the most brilliant and extraordinary person anyone had ever met. He simply had the misfortune to live at the same time as his much younger cousin, Cúchulainn. Conall had a connection to the Otherworld that showed up in his physical appearance: One side of his face was freckled, and the other half pale and smooth as milk. The eye on his freckled side was blue; the other black as a beetle-shell. And his hair was so magnificently thick and curly that if a bushel of berries were emptied over his head, not one of them would touch the ground.

THE STORY YOU NEED TO KNOW

Conall Cearnach's mother, Findchoem, was sister to both the king of Ulster and a great warrior of Connaught called Cet (pronounced "ket"). Findchoem married the poet Amergin, but the couple were

barren, until Findchoem sought druidic advice. She drank the water from a healing well, which contained a tiny insect (a common trope in Otherworldly conceptions), and became pregnant. She went to where Cet was in Connaught for the duration of her pregnancy, where he took care of her.

As soon as the baby was born, a druid made a prophecy that he would grow up to be a mighty warrior...of Ulster. He also said that the baby would kill more Connaught men than were alive on that day, and that no Connaught man would kill him. Cet (his uncle) felt so strongly about the rivalry between provinces that he immediately tried to murder his newborn nephew by stepping on his neck, but true to the druid's word, the child could not be killed by a Connaught man, and Conall simply had a crooked neck for the rest of his life.

The rest of the prophecy came true as well. Conall became a brutally brilliant warrior, his forked beard striking fear into all warriors of Connaught. For a time, he was said to only be able to sleep if he had a freshly severed Connaught head under his knee. His position of border guard of Ulster put him into contact with plenty of Connaught raiders to accomplish this, and he honored his king by giving out payments to poets as they were leaving the province to make sure they had enjoyed their time there.

Conall's rivalry with Cet of Connaught rumbled on for years, owning in no small part to the crooked neck he received from his uncle at birth, but it was Conall's rivalry with Cúchulainn, the hound, that has kept his story alive.

Conall is central in the tale of the Champion's Portion. King Conchobar was reluctant to appoint the champion of Ulster, an important position, because he was mindful of the large and fragile egos of warriors. Cúchulainn was a surprisingly controversial choice, as he was considered too young, too daring, and too beautiful to be declared champion.

The rivalry for the coveted position of champion came to a boiling point between Conall and Cúchulainn at a feast thrown by Bricriu of the Bitter Tongue, who provoked an argument over who should be named the champion of Ulster for his own amusement.

King Conchobar refused to decide who would get the champion title, because he knew that whoever was *not* named champion would have a grudge against him. He sent Conall, Cúchulainn, and a third warrior, Lóegaire (who was mostly there for comedic relief), away to be judged elsewhere so that he would not be blamed by the disappointed warriors. Queen Medb was asked to judge between the contenders for this title, and she set various tests for Conall, Cúchulainn, and Lóegaire. King Conchobar secretly hoped that she'd have to deal with the ensuing fight.

Medb's clever solution was to give each man a test at night, and then to present each privately with a precious cup and tell them to produce it at the next feast. Only when they were back in Ulster did they present the cups and see that Lóegaire's was bronze, Conall's was silver, and Cúchulainn's was gold. Medb had cleverly chosen Cúchulainn but avoided bloodshed on her ground. The results, however, were still disputed, with Conall and Lóegaire insisting that Cúchulainn must have slept with Medb—which would not have been out of character for either of them.

None of the three warriors would drop the dispute until their king announced who was the true champion. In another attempt to avoid making a decision, King Conchobar sent them to Munster to be similarly tested by a powerful sorcerer named Cú Roi Mac Dáire. A powerful person from outside of Ulster was seen as a neutral judge, and Cú Roi's power meant that the two warriors who were not chosen might not attack him. The sorcerer was absent but had still set impossible tests for the would-be champions, and only Cúchulainn was able to pass these. Once more, the judgment wasn't accepted, and Conall stubbornly claimed that Cúchulainn must have had help from the Otherworld.

A stranger then offered the would-be champions a final test: They could behead him with his own axe, but on the following day, he would return to behead them. Lóegaire volunteered first, thinking the man mad, and was suitably shocked to see the headless body stand back up again. Lóegaire's nerve broke and he fled, so Conall volunteered when the stranger started to insult the honor of all of Ulster. He tried to chop the head into small pieces, but this ploy did not work, and to his horror, the headless stranger also stood up and picked up his axe expectantly. Conall fled as well. Only Cúchulainn was willing to put his own head on the executioner's block for the honor of his province. The stranger revealed himself to be Cú Roi Mac Dáire. He admonished the other two warriors, saying that if they ever felt like arguing over the champion position any further, they could come to him.

Conall and Cúchulainn made peace and made a pact to avenge one another's deaths, should one of them die without any sons to do the job. Conall indeed avenged Cúchulainn's death, killing the man who killed the hound with one hand tied behind his back. He even defeated his long-standing rival, Cet, though not before Cet dealt Conchobar Mac Nessa's death blow.

In the end, Conall grew old. Cantankerous, sick with leprosy, and no longer able to fight, he was forced to retire to Connaught, where only Medb and her consort Ailill were wealthy enough to afford to feed his still-prodigious appetite. A sad end for a warrior who was too fierce to have died in any battle he fought in, but still desired to have a hero's death in battle.

One day, Medb caught Ailill with a serving girl (their open relationship was strictly one-sided—only Medb could have other partners) and asked Conall to teach him a lesson. Instead, Conall murdered Ailill in the middle of the feasting hall and ran away back to Ulster. Every warrior in Connaught pursued him, catching up to him at a river crossing. He was drowned—not by any *one* Connaught man, but by all of them at once... thus proving his birth prophecy to be true.

Now You Know

The second greatest warrior of Ulster, after Cúchulainn, was Cúchulainn's friend and mildly psychotic, yet hugely loyal, cousin Conall. The beheading test is a trope that also appears in Arthurian legend, famously in the story of Sir Gawain and the Green Knight. Scholars agree that the Irish version is older and seems to have originated the test.

MEDB

PRONUNCIATION: MAYV

ALSO KNOWN AS: MAEVE, MEDHBH, THE ONE WHO INTOXICATES

Daughter of Eochaid Feidlech (High King of Ireland) and Cruacha (woman-king of Connaught), Medb was destined for power. She was known for her courage, generosity, and beauty, which had a profound effect on men. Her name, Medb, means "intoxicating," and may share an etymological root with the word "mead." She is described as fair-haired, long faced, and so beautiful that she robbed men of two-thirds of their courage. She used her beauty to her advantage and often "intoxicated" men with promises of wealth, land, and the friendship of her thighs if they did her bidding. (Most did.) Those who didn't met the harsh nature of this formidable and ruthless ruler.

Medb is heavily villainized in many retellings of the Ulster Cycle. She comes under particular fire for aspects of her personality that became culturally unacceptable. For example, Medb's promiscuity was a sign of potency in the ancient world, but it was a sign of immorality in the Christian era. Similarly, her skill as a warrior and tactician, which was a prerequisite for a ruler in ancient Ireland, became a sign of perversion of the "nature" of a woman in later reinterpretations.

THE STORY YOU NEED TO KNOW

When she was a young woman, Medb's father asked her to marry the handsome, ambitious king of Ulster, Conchobar Mac Nessa, and Medb did see a potential equal partner in him. Unfortunately, their marriage was a disaster, perhaps due to Medb's sexual appetite meshing poorly with Conchobar's jealousy.

After their divorce, Medb's eternal enmity for Conchobar was cemented when he caught her bathing by the River Boyne after an assembly at Tara. Having left her weapons on the bank, she was alone and vulnerable, and he sexually assaulted her.

Medb later won the leadership of Connaught, where her mother had built the fort at Crúachan Aí, right at the edge of a passage to the Otherworld. Leadership was not inherited in ancient Ireland, and those with an ancestral claim to a particular territory had to fight for it. Medb won the leadership of Connaught by deposing the then-king of Connaught, Tinni Mac Conri. She and Tinni later became lovers, and he regained a degree of control over the province. Tinni fought a duel with Conchobar Mac Nessa when Tinni tried to avenge the insult to Medb's honor and person that Conchobar had committed, but Conchobar was victorious and killed Tinni. Medb then took another lover as her co-regent, Eochaid Dála.

Medb had a special connection to the Otherworldly powers and to this specific portal between worlds called Oweynagat, or The Cave of Cats, where she could call creatures forth. She did this to test the Ulster champions (see Conall Cearnach's entry), calling giant catlike creatures to attack the would-be champions, to see who would fare best.

Medb was also called upon many times to mediate incursions from the Otherworld in the form of strange weather and even stranger creatures. Once, an entire plain of Connaught was infested with pigs that ate everything that grew for a whole year. Medb had to banish the pigs back to the Otherworld by counting them—literally: one, two, three—to save the people there from starvation.

Queen Medb famously never had a man in bed without another man waiting outside. She remarried several times and made each husband

swear that he would be as brave as her, be as generous as her, and have no jealousy. Her third husband, Eochaid Dála, struggled with the non-jealousy vow when Medb started a passionate relationship with her bodyguard, Ailill. Eochaid Dála fought a duel with Ailill, losing both duel and life. She eventually settled down with Ailill.

Medb had seven sons and asked a druid which one would kill Conchobar. When he replied "Maine," she renamed all seven sons Maine. The prophecy later turned out to refer to a different king entirely—a Scottish king who was coincidentally also named Conchobar (remember, in ancient times, there were multiple kings of different provinces, counties, and countries). So, none of her sons killed Conchobar, though Conchobar was responsible for her son Maine Mórgor's death. Medb exacted her vengeance for the death of her son by killing two of Conchobar's sons in retaliation.

Medb was a very skilled warrior, and she cut a fine figure on her way into battle. She has been described as being dressed in a golden headdress, with a chariot on either side and one in front (to keep the dust and mud from blemishing her gown), and with a songbird on her shoulder. She wielded a spear, which burst into flames when she called upon her battle rage.

One morning, Medb and Ailill had their most famous quarrel, a tale known as "The Pillow Talk." What started as a lighthearted teasing about which of them was luckier to be married to the other became a deadly serious power struggle. In a culture that counted wealth by head of cattle, the difference between them ultimately came down to a single bull—which Medb had, ironically, given to Ailill as a gift. To restore balance between them, Medb sought out the equal of the bull, finding only one in all of Ireland, and it was in Cooley…in the territory of Ulster, their greatest rival.

After failing to secure a peaceful purchase of the enormous Brown Bull of Cooley, Medb assembled a huge army drawn from all over Ireland, including the Exiles of Ulster (the entry called Fergus Mac Róich has more on that topic). She wanted to lead this army to Ulster in the greatest cattle raid in Irish myth, called *Táin Bó Cúailnge*, or *The Cattle Raid of Cooley*. On the eve of departing Connaught and marching northeast across Ireland with this huge army, she received a prophecy from a woman of the Otherworld, who said of Medb's army: "I see them all crimson; I see them all red." She also said that Medb would win the Brown Bull and return safely–but at a terrible cost.

The cost was indeed terrible, and despite the size of their army and the lack of fighting resistance from the armies of Ulster (see Fergus Mac Róich's entry for more on the curse of Macha that explains this), the Ulster hero Cúchulainn stood alone against her raiders. He waged guerrilla-style warfare against the army at night, attacking from hiding. He killed hundreds before eventually agreeing to fight single combats against Medb's chosen champions (see Cúchulainn's entry for more on these battles). He succeeded in slowing the army down until the Red Branch warriors awoke from their curse and drove the invaders out of Ulster.

Medb lost two of her sons and her daughter Finnabair, as well as countless allies. In the end, it was a Pyrrhic victory, and although she successfully stole the Brown Bull of Cooley, when she arrived back home in Connaught, the prized bulls destroyed each other.

In later years, Medb showed her persistence. Knowing the downfall of Cúchulainn would lead to Ulster's demise, she gathered another army out of all the relatives of the warriors Cúchulainn had killed during the *Táin* and successfully led them to take his life and end Ulster's golden age.

Toward the end of her life, Medb retired to an island on Lough Rea (a lake not far from present-day Galway), where she was assassinated by her nephew, who believed that Medb had killed his mother long ago. She was killed with a piece of cheese shot from a sling, which seems an odd choice for a missile.

Medb is said to have been buried on her feet, standing upright and facing Ulster, eternally vigilant against her enemies. Her legacy is so significant that several communities in northwest Ireland claim to be the site of her final resting place. In County Sligo, northwest Ireland, it is said that her grave lies at a cairn in Knocknarea called Queen Maeve's Cairn. A little farther south in Galway, they claim she is resting under the ancient cairn on the oak-forested hill of Cnoc Meadha (or Knockma), which also bears her name. Meanwhile, in the village of Tulsk in County Roscommon, in between Sligo and Galway, locals are convinced that Medb's final resting place is where she once had her seat of power and ruled from: Crúachan Aí, or Rathcroghan as it is known today.

Now You Know

Queen Maeve, a character in the TV show and comic book series The Boys, likely takes inspiration from Medb. Beautiful, sensual, powerful, and terrible, Medb is the epitome of the warrior queen, mediator with the forces of the Otherworld, and a woman you most certainly do not want as an enemy. She may hearken back to older Irish sovereignty goddesses, such as another goddess called Medb Lethderg, who may have been an earlier incarnation of Queen Medb. Images of Medb on her chariot and more medieval evidence for the existence of her ruling from the west can be seen in the visitors' center in Tulsk at Rathcroghan, an archaeological site. Medb also remains a popular name in Ireland to this day, often modernized in spelling as "Maeve."

CONCHOBAR MAC NESSA

Pronunciation: CRU-HOOR MAC NESS-A
Also Known As: Connor, King of Ulster

The king of Ulster during the Ulster Cycle and the *Táin* (Cattle Raid), Conchobar is cast in a heroic role as a great king in most adaptations. Becoming king of Ulster at this time also meant he was the leader of the *Craobh Rua*, or the Red Branch warriors of Ulster, which were the greatest and most feared group of warriors in Ireland at the time. And though they were fierce, much of the characterization of Conchobar as a great king was due to Christian transcribers likening him to Christ. After all, he was born on the same day as Christ, and due to the manner of Conchobar's death (on the day of Christ's crucifixion!), he was said to be the only pagan ever to gain access to heaven.

On closer inspection, he was a pretty terrible king, as almost every important decision Conchobar made seems to have exacerbated situations he was in. These bad decisions ultimately paved the way for the destruction of the Red Branch and the downfall of Ulster's golden age of dominance in Ireland.

Egocentric, prideful, and obsessed with his own image and legacy, he would more accurately be known as the "king of how to make things worse."

THE STORY YOU NEED TO KNOW

Conchobar grew up to be a famously beautiful man: tall, golden-haired, and with calves so beautiful that the women of Ulster made a new law that it was illegal for him to wear a long tunic and cover them, even in the depths of winter. He gladly obliged.

After becoming the king of Ulster through his mother's clever deal-making, he solidified his kingship using her advice. In the early years of his kingship, he had a disastrous marriage with Medb, the daughter of the High King. After a tumultuous marriage, Medb left him and Conchobar held a bitter grudge for the insult; he ultimately sexually assaulted her on the banks of the River Boyne, solidifying their eternal enmity toward each other.

The young king Conchobar also forced what he thought was a heavily pregnant woman to run a footrace against his new team of chariot horses after a separate insult, dealt this time by the woman's husband. She turned out to be a heavily pregnant *goddess* in disguise (see the Rhiannon & Macha entry for this story). She miscarried her twins after winning the race, and in a fury, she revealed herself to be a goddess and cursed the men of Ulster for nine generations in retribution. From the time they were able to grow a beard on their chin, any time the province was attacked, all of the fighters would be struck down by the pains of a woman in childbirth for nine days and nine nights, needing a nine-day sleep to recover. This curse became Ulster's greatest-kept secret, and Conchobar's greatest mistake. Until…

A prophecy came to light that a then-unborn child (see the Deirdre entry for the full tale) was going to be the most beautiful woman in the world, and the rivalry over who would get to be with her would tear the Red Branch warriors asunder. Conchobar proclaimed that the girl, Deirdre, would be raised in isolation, and married to him when she came of age. He would put her in such a high status as his wife that no man would dare challenge him for her. This would have worked out perfectly if the child in question had absolutely no will of her own.

Despite setting in motion the tragedy of Deirdre, and drawing the ire of a goddess and a queen, Conchobar also made some good decisions. He set up the Boys-Troop of Emain Macha as a place to train young warriors, and made sure to pay poets handsomely, so that they could spread word of Ulster's power.

When the young Deirdre grew up, she ran away to Scotland with another man and his two brothers (known as the Sons of Uisneach). Conchobar's jealousy got the better of him, and he declared them outcasts, placing a price on their heads. Eventually, years later, and after many begged him to forgive and forget, Conchobar tricked his predecessor, Fergus Mac Róich, into bringing Deirdre and the three brothers home under the pretense of forgiveness. Ulster's druid, Cathbad, threatened Conchobar that none of his five sons would be king after him if *he* killed the Sons of Uisneach. But Conchobar's jealousy and self-righteous attitude did not abate, and he had a mercenary from Munster do the evil deed of killing the Sons of Uisneach, hoping that because he technically did not do the evil murderous deed himself that Cathbad's prophetic warning would not come to pass. This attempt at having someone else swing the sword to kill the three brothers, however, did not exempt him from the druid's curse.

After a bloody battle that split the Red Branch in two, Fergus and half of the remaining Red Branch warriors left Ulster forever, including one of Conchobar's own sons, Cormac.

Much later, Queen Medb led an enormous cattle raid against Ulster, called the *Táin Bó Cúailgne*. Because of Conchobar's betrayal of the Sons of Uisneach and Fergus's desertion to Connaught, Medb had the insider information of the curse's existence and knew that her invasion would trigger the curse. Thus, two of Conchobar's great mistakes set the stage for the terrible invasion. By the time the *Táin* took place, Cúchulainn had become the champion of Ulster and was able to resist the army single-handedly.

Yet another prophecy haunted Conchobar. He was told that if Ulster's champion were to die in battle, Ulster would be without luck forever. And the champion of Ulster was now the famously reckless Cúchulainn. Though Cúchulainn survived the events of the *Táin*, and fought in many great battles subsequently, Queen Medb amassed a new army years later with the specific goal of killing Ulster's champion.

Conchobar did his best to try and hide the invasion from Cúchulainn, distracting him with feasts, hiding the pain of the curse of Macha from him, and sending him to a magical valley that let in no sound from the outside world. But Conchobar failed, and Cúchulainn went to his death willingly.

Conchobar's end was convoluted. The great rival of Conall Cearnach, Cet of Connaught, hit Conchobar in the head with a slingshot. The shot did not go deep enough to kill him, but lodged precariously in his skull. Healers could not remove it, so they stitched it in place with golden thread to match his hair. He was instructed to give up all alcohol and to never lose his temper, ride a horse, or make love. He lived for seven years with this enforced temperance.

One day, the sky darkened, and Cathbad the druid explained that this was happening because an innocent man was being killed horribly in Palestine. Conchobar flew into a rage, proclaiming that he would go there himself to defend this man. He rode on horseback to the coast, and the buildup of pressure made the slingshot fly out of his head, drenching him in his own blood as he died. Thus, it was said by Christian monks that Conchobar was the only pagan ever to enter heaven, as he died in a baptism of blood while thinking only of Christ.

FERGUS MAC RÓICH

PRONUNCIATION: FIR-gus Mc Roy
ALSO KNOWN AS: THE CHAMPION OF ULSTER

Fergus Mac Róich was not known for being a wise king of Ulster, but he was a wonderfully loyal, proud, fierce warrior with a sword so large it looked like the oar of a boat hanging from his hip as he approached. His immense stature is often referred to in descriptions—his bushy hair, broad shoulders, and emerald cloak loomed above others around him, giving him the appearance of a large oak tree in a forest. Fergus was famous for his prowess, both on the battlefield and in the bedroom.

Though he was a principled man of deep conviction and a strict honor code, his choices led him from being Ulster's king to leading an invading army against his former home, all to enact vengeance for a broken oath. Though steadfast in his action, he was continually outmaneuvered by the more savvy politicians, Medb of Connaught and Conchobar of Ulster. As Cúchulainn's foster father and trainer, Fergus provided some of the only fatherly attention offered to the young hero Cúchulainn. Seen as having a good and noble heart, Fergus offers an empathic insight into the tumultuous difficulties of loyalty and the difficulties of being true to one's word absolutely.

THE STORY YOU NEED TO KNOW

Fergus's huge sword, called Caladbolg (Hard Dinter), was so big that it cut a rainbow across the sky when it was drawn, and could cut the tops off mountains in a single blow. Fergus was nicknamed "Fergus of the Horses," though he was not particularly good with animals. Fergus's sexual appetite was legendary, and it was said that he needed to sleep with seven women in one day to stay satisfied.

As a young man, Fergus was elected king of Ulster, a province that valued martial skill. Kingship didn't really suit the straightforward Fergus, who was not a politically minded person and was not able to navigate the cross-currents of shifting alliances within his kingdom. When he met Nessa, he was happy to meet her bride price by allowing her son to take the throne for a year. When her young son fully supplanted him, Fergus didn't seem to mind too much. It suited him better to train the Boys-Troop and claim the honored position of champion of Ulster, which came with the best cut of meat at every feast.

Fergus was one of Cúchulainn's foster fathers and instilled his devout loyalty in his foster son. As a result, his life took a dramatic turn when a young warrior called Naoise, whom he had mentored and trained, ran away with King Conchobar's betrothed, Deirdre. Fergus couldn't quite understand Conchobar's rage and tried for years to talk him into letting Naoise and his brothers (known as the Sons of Uisneach) come home. When the king finally agreed to forgive and forget the past, Fergus excitedly traveled to Scotland to retrieve Deirdre and the Sons of Uisneach.

Conchobar had sworn to Fergus that he would not kill the Sons of Uisneach but had invited a mercenary army from Munster to stay in Emain Macha on the night they were to arrive.

On their way back to Emain Macha with the Sons of Uisneach, Fergus was tactfully delayed but feared nothing. He had the king's word the young men would be safe when they went ahead and arrived without him. But by the time he got to Emain Macha, Fergus found it in flames. The three headless bodies of the Sons of Uisneach lay beside one of his own sons, killed defending them and his father's word. Fergus realized that this was not the work of invaders but a calculated plot by his own king, who had used him to bring the brothers back under a false promise of safety, deliberately had him waylaid, and ordered one of the mercenary warriors to murder them.

Disgusted, Fergus left right away, taking half of the Red Branch with him. Fergus and the Exiles of Ulster went straight to Connaught and pledged loyalty to Queen Medb, Conchobar's greatest enemy, swearing he would do whatever it took to face Conchobar on the battlefield and avenge the Sons of Uisneach, and his own murdered son.

In Medb, Fergus found both a leader and the great love of his life. Her sexual appetite was as famous as his own, and they found they could keep up with one another where no one else could. Medb's fondness for Fergus was so pronounced that it provoked jealousy in her husband and consort, Ailill. In what seems like a very Freudian move, he went so far as to steal Fergus's great sword, a weakness Fergus concealed by carving a wooden sword to keep in his scabbard (to make it still seem like he had Caladbolg) and avoiding having to draw the blade.

Fergus decided to reveal Conchobar's greatest secret to Medb—he told her all about the curse of Macha (which caused the warriors of Ulster to lose their strength whenever they needed it most) and Ulster's long-hidden vulnerability. This was the last excuse Medb needed to raid Ulster for the Brown Bull of Cooley.

Fergus's loyalties were always divided, as his personal vendetta against Conchobar (which led him to side with Connaught) never overshadowed his love for his native province (Ulster). He was put in charge of Medb's army but led them astray to give the Ulster warriors a chance to recover from their curse. He also hid the fact that Cúchulainn, who was capable of single-handedly fighting off small armies, was exempt from the curse.

During the *Táin*, and in the early days of crossing the Ulster border, Fergus witnessed Cúchulainn's guerrilla tactics against the vast army with a mixture of pride and fear. Fergus reluctantly agreed to fight

Cúchulainn at the ford, but he was quick to make a deal with his former protégé: If Cúchulainn ran from him in single combat, he would run from Cúchulainn the next time they met in battle.

In the final battle of the *Táin*, Fergus saw his chance to strike Conchobar down, but a wounded Cúchulainn rose up from his sickbed to intervene. Ever honorable, Fergus gave up his chance at revenge, turned his sword on the nearby mountains, flattened their tops with a single blow, and fled. He failed to consider that, as he was the general of the army, his fleeing sent a message to the troops: All of Medb's army of Ireland broke when they saw Fergus run, and the invaders were chased out of Ulster.

In the end, Fergus died as he had lived: having loud public sex with Queen Medb. Medb's husband, Ailill, tricked his blind brother into thinking that there were two deer mating in the water, and the blind hunter's cast felled the great Fergus. A straightforward man embroiled in a complex power struggle, Fergus always put honor before everything, sacrificing his home, and his chance at revenge, holding others to the same high standards he had for himself.

DEIRDRE

PRONUNCIATION: DEER-DRUH
**ALSO KNOWN AS: DEIRDRIU, DEIRDRE OF THE SORROWS,
THE MOST BEAUTIFUL WOMAN IN THE WORLD**

In Irish tradition, there are said to be three great "sorrows of storytelling." The Children of Lir is a famous tale of persecuted children transformed into swans; the Sons of Tuireann tells of three brothers who were sent on a doomed quest by Lugh; and the third is this story. Deirdre is doomed from the start. Beautiful, wild, and willful, she also represents a thread in the tapestry of the Ulster Cycle, as the repercussions of her actions, and the revenge taken against her, had far-reaching implications.

THE STORY YOU NEED TO KNOW

Deirdre grew up in isolation, with only two points of human contact: her nurse, Leabharcham, who was a poet and satirist; and an old, mute man who would sometimes do chores for them.

Leabharcham educated young Deirdre as best she could in their hidden valley. But Deirdre grew up lonely, wishing for the company of people her own age. From time to time, her nurse would go away, returning with fresh provisions and fresh stories of Emain Macha, the king of Ulster's fort.

One winter's day, when Deirdre was on the threshold of womanhood, the old, mute man butchered a calf, and a raven flew down to peck at the bloodstains on the snow. Deirdre gasped in shock, struck by a sudden prophetic vision. She declared then and there that she would only love a man with those colors on him: raven-black hair; snow-white body; blood-red cheeks.

Leabharcham recognized the ring of a prophecy in her words and tried to undo what had just been put into motion. She told Deirdre that she was already betrothed—to the king! She also had to confess that the king, while famously handsome, was fair-haired.

Deirdre scoffed at the idea of marrying a king, caring nothing for Leabharcham's descriptions of the high social status she would have—after all, why would a child raised in the wilderness care about or understand high rank?

Instead, she pestered her nurse to tell her if there was a man out there with the coloring she'd seen on that winter day. Leabharcham resisted as long as she could, but eventually confessed that there was a handsome young warrior of Ulster called Naoise, son of Uisneach, who fit the bill. Deirdre now pestered Leabharcham constantly to arrange for her to catch a glimpse of Naoise.

Unable to resist Deirdre for long, Leabharcham dropped a word in the ear of Naoise and his brothers that there was fine hunting near the hidden valley where Deirdre lived. The three Sons of Uisneach took the bait, and they soon went hunting, singing in perfect three-part harmony as they went.

Deirdre promised not to talk to the hunters, but the promise went out the window as soon as she saw the man of her dreams. She stepped out in front of Naoise, blushing so deeply that her beauty became even more radiant. Naoise knew exactly who she was.

Before her birth, a druid had prophesied that she would be the most beautiful woman in the world, and that her beauty would be her curse, causing conflict among the warriors of Ulster and ultimately dividing the Red Branch. It was for this reason she grew up in the wilderness. And all knew that one day she would be married to the king, to prevent anyone else from claiming her as their own.

Naoise's heart was well and truly claimed by Deirdre nonetheless. The two quickly resolved to run away together. Naoise's older brothers, Ainnle and Ardan, were determined to go with the lovers to protect them, and Leabharcham promised to keep the elopement a secret as long as she could.

They fled to Scotland, where the three brothers fought in the army of the king of Scotland for a time. They had to keep Deirdre hidden miserably away in a little house (confined again!) while they fought by day and joined her in the evenings. The king found out about the beautiful woman that the Irishmen were concealing and decided he should have her for himself. He attempted to have them killed by putting the three brothers on the front line of every battle.

Deirdre realized what was going on and persuaded the brothers to flee again. This time, they settled in the wilderness of the Scottish Highlands together. Here, at last, away from jealous eyes, Deirdre could be truly free. She was no longer confined to the small spaces she'd had to grow used to. She bore several children, who were given to the sea king, Manannán Mac Lir, to raise in the Otherworld. Naoise was given Manannán's exceptional sword to protect Deirdre and his two brothers with. They lived peacefully for years, until the former king of Ulster (and the man who had trained the Sons of Uisneach as warriors) Fergus Mac Róich came with an offer of reconciliation. King Conchobar of Ulster had finally agreed to forgive the Sons of Uisneach for taking Deirdre away and had promised Fergus that he would not harm them and would allow them all to return and take up their place as warriors of the Red Branch of Ulster.

Deirdre's prophetic gift returned, bringing her dreams of honeyed words turning into blood, and nightmares of smoke and violence. She wanted to stay in Scotland, but Naoise and his brothers desperately missed their home and had not enjoyed the wilderness nearly so much as Deirdre. She was overruled, and they all returned to Ireland under Fergus's protection.

When Fergus was called away—or tricked, some would say—Deirdre knew their doom was certain. Despite Fergus ordering his two sons to protect the brothers in his stead, she was correct. The first son was bribed to betray his father, Fergus, and the second would die defending his word.

And so, Conchobar broke his promise to Fergus and surrounded the group. He ordered a mercenary from Munster, Maine Rough Hand, to murder the brothers, beheading them with Naoise's own sword in a single blow.

The broken-hearted Deirdre was kept as Conchobar's prisoner for a year, as he attempted to win her over. Eventually frustrated, he decided to send her off to live with Maine Rough Hand, the man who had swung the sword that killed her beloved—in other words, the only man who she hated fractionally more than Conchobar.

On the way to be delivered into this even greater misery, Deirdre leaned out of the speeding chariot and dashed her head off on an overhanging rock, ending her suffering and reuniting her with her beloved in the Otherworld.

Now You Know

Deirdre's tragedy has a high place in Irish literature, inspiring many retellings. It has even inspired paintings! Like the tragic Greek prophet Cassandra, whose true visions were doomed to be dismissed, Deirdre's plight made her a popular character. During Ireland's colonization, she became a symbol of oppression, endlessly passive, endlessly victimized. More recent retellings have attempted to give her back some degree of agency and autonomy.

FIONN MAC CUMHAILL

PRONUNCIATION: FIN ma-KOOL, FYUN ma-KOOL
ALSO KNOWN AS: FINN MAC CUMHAILL, FIND MAC UMAILL, FEUNN MAC CÜAIL, FINN MAC COOL, DEIMNE (CHILDHOOD NAME)

Fionn Mac Cumhaill, leader of a band of warriors called the Fianna, is one of the greatest and most famous heroes of Irish and Scottish myth. A *fian* (singular) was a kind of extended spring break for late adolescent/early adult warriors, after they finished their fosterage and before they took up their duties in their families of origin. This was part of the training for warriors, as they were expected to fend for themselves during the summer months: hunting, fishing, and living off the land between Bealtaine (in early May) and Samhain (Halloween).

The Fianna (plural of *fian*) of myth was an idealization of this kind of life, and Fionn Mac Cumhaill led them in their glory days, defending Ireland from invaders from overseas as well as threats from the Otherworld. There is a saying among storytellers that the day that the name of Fionn Mac Cumhaill is not spoken aloud will be the day the world ends, because on that day, humanity will have forgotten everything that is important.

THE STORY YOU NEED TO KNOW

Fionn's story spans many legends. His father, Cumhall, was killed by another member of the Fianna, Goll Mac Morna, while Fionn's mother,

Muirne, was pregnant, and she left him to be raised in secret by (lesbian power couple) Bodhmall and Liath Luachra.

Originally named Deimne (meaning "little deer"), he grew up outside of society to protect him from Goll's wrath. The son of a warrior who was killed in battle would be expected to grow up and avenge his father's killing. It would have been in Goll's best interests to kill the child of Cumhall before he could grow up to become a threat to Goll. As he grew up, his existence became harder to hide, and eventually, the young boy was apprenticed to poets. It was the poets who named him Fionn, which means "fair-haired," the name he became famous for.

After his initial apprenticeship, Fionn wanted to know more. Filled with questions, he sought out the wisest man in Ireland, the great poet Finnegas, who was obsessed with catching the Salmon of Knowledge. The first person to taste its flesh would gain all the knowledge of this world and the Otherworld. Finnegas fished in the Boyne (if the storyteller is from the east of Ireland) or the Shannon (if they're from the west). Young Fionn became his assistant, cooking and cleaning for the old man, ensuring that he had clean clothes and warm food. At last, Finnegas caught the mystical salmon, but Fionn burned his thumb on the side of the fish as he was cooking it. Putting his thumb into his mouth to cool it, he unwittingly stole the first, magical taste of the fish.

Fionn went on to win the leadership of the Fianna from Goll Mac Morna by defeating the fire-breathing faery musician called Aillén Mac Midgna, who burned the High King's hall at Tara every Samhain. Aillén had thwarted all attempts by Goll Mac Morna and the Fianna to stop him, because he played magical music that lulled all the listeners to sleep before setting the hall alight. Fionn kept himself awake using the poisonous fumes of a magical spear to counteract the enchanted lullaby and drove Aillén away. As a reward for his services, and because he had done what Goll could not, Fionn was made captain of the Fianna. He

made peace with Goll, who swore fealty to Fionn, cementing his place as a wise leader and bringing the Fianna into a golden age.

Fionn made the entry tests for joining the Fianna more physically strenuous, and he demanded that aspirants learn to recite and make poems…but he also made entry open to all who wished to try, where previously the Fianna had only been open to those of the warrior class. Their motto was "strength of limb, purity of heart, and actions to match our words."

Over his years as leader of the Fianna, the tales of Fionn are numerous, often episodic, and relatively disconnected. These tales include: adventures to the Otherworld, where Fionn and a faithful/recurring cohort learn some Otherworldly lesson or knowledge; tragic tales of love and loss; strange companions who turn up and offer to serve the Fianna (and usually turn out to be from the Otherworld); and epic tales of battles against incredible odds or monstrous creatures. At times, Fionn and the Fianna came into direct conflict with the king of Ireland (see the entry on Caoilte for that story); at other times, they served him as a standing army. Eventually, Fionn and the High King's relationship broke down when the High King's daughter, Gráinne, left Fionn at the altar.

Gráinne's brother Cairbre Lifechair became the next High King, and he was determined to break the Fianna's power. With Fionn's son Oisín away in the Otherworld, things were looking bleak. The Battle of Gabhra put an end to the Fianna's power once and for all.

Fionn himself is said to have had three deaths: One at the Battle of Gabhra with so many of his companions. Another story has it that he left Ireland, going to sleep under the hills of the Otherworld, waiting to be called on again in a time of Ireland's need. Yet another story tells that as Fionn grew older, he tested himself every year. He found a ford on the River Boyne with a narrow ledge on each side. By gathering all of his strength, he was just about able to leap from one cliff to the other. Rather than gradually decline in power, he would fall at the first weakening of his body. And some say that's exactly what happened.

Now You Know

Some people call him Finn; others, Fionn (pronounced "fyun" or "fee-yun")—both are acceptable and still refer to the fearless leader of the Fianna. Fionn Mac Cumhaill is one of the greatest heroes in Ireland's mythological tapestry. The Giant's Causeway, a popular tourist attraction in County Antrim on the north coast of Northern Ireland, takes its name from a Fionn story, where a Scottish giant built a stone causeway (or land bridge) to Ireland to fight Fionn. The giant was scared away by the stories he heard about Fionn, however, so he ripped up the stones and threw them back over his shoulder, where they all neatly landed together in County Antrim. Some will have you believe it's a geological phenomenon caused by prehistoric volcanic rock. However, we know it's because of Fionn.

Fionn's inspiration has rippled throughout history, and his influence appears in everything from traditional retellings to modern takes via comics, in songs from somber ballads to rock anthems…and approximately every third Irish pub in the world is named after him!

LIATH LUACHRA & BODHMALL

PRONUNCIATION: LEE-A LOO-KRA; BOW-MAL

Though they are best remembered for their role in raising the great hero Fionn Mac Cumhaill, both Bodhmall (a druid) and Liath Luachra (a warrior) were formidable characters in their own right. Liath Luachra's name crops up several times in the Fianna Cycle and seems to refer to several different characters. But it's not disputed that Liath Luachra raised Fionn and taught him how to fight. Bodhmall and Liath Luachra's story is very open to queer readings, and there is nothing in the oldest version of the story to refute the idea that they shared a romantic connection.

THE STORY YOU NEED TO KNOW

When Bodhmall's brother, Cumhall, was killed by a rival over the leadership of the Fianna, he left behind a pregnant lover, Muirne. Her family had already cast her out over the affair with the warrior Cumhall, so Bodhmall stepped in to take care of the young woman. Both knew that Cumhall's rivals would not want a child of his to grow to adulthood and potentially seek revenge. As long as Muirne was pregnant, her life was at risk.

Bodhmall attended the young woman until her labor came on her. Bodhmall's husband fended off Cumhall's enemies as they turned up at the door, giving his life to delay them. When the enemies finally entered the house, they found an exhausted Muirne, no longer with child—but there was also no sign of Bodhmall or the infant. Bodhmall had brought the boy to the Slieve Bloom Mountains, where she could keep him secret and raise him alone.

Unexpectedly, she was discovered, but not by one of Cumhall's rivals. Instead, a loyal follower of his—Liath Luachra—turned up in the woods to help. As a former member of the Fianna, Liath Luachra was a ferocious protector, a brilliant warrior, and someone who was an expert at living off the land.

The two women lived together, raising the child as they saw fit. They named him Deimne, which means "little deer." Bodhmall would send him into the forest alone to watch the birds and animals and then tell her what lessons he could learn from them—such as cunning from the fox, patience from the wolf, alertness from the deer, cooperation from the ant, and resilience from the salmon.

Liath Luachra's curriculum was more physical. She taught Deimne how to swim by throwing him into cold water and letting him find his own way out, until finally he was swimming like a fish. She taught him how to fight with sticks by chasing him around and around a huge tree. The lesson was concluded when he managed to catch up with her and land a blow. She further honed his skills as a warrior with games of skill and strength.

At night, the three of them would gather around the fire, exchanging stories and songs.

The boy's mother, Muirne, came to visit just once, while he was sleeping. She sang songs to him, stroked his hair, and left before he woke.

As the boy Deimne grew up, he began to sneak away to play hurling (a traditional Irish game) with children his own age. Bodhmall and Liath Luachra realized that this isolated life was coming to an end, but they also understood that the boy was still at risk if his identity should become known. They did not want to send Deimne out into the world unprotected, so they apprenticed him to a group of traveling poets. The killing or harming of poets was seen as a deep sacrilege, so they knew that this plan would keep the boy safe from his father's enemies. The poets took Deimne in, so struck by his fair hair that they nicknamed him "Fionn," which means "fair-haired" (clearly, the nickname stuck).

Bodhmall and Liath Luachra had sent the boy out into the world to make his own way but found that they had come to love their quiet life in the mountains, with only each other for company. So there they stayed.

Now You Know

This is one of many Irish stories of women holding positions that might not be considered "traditionally feminine," but female druids and warriors are *not* rare in Irish myth. Druidic rituals and rites were considered too important to write down. The belief was that stories that are written down can be forgotten, and sadly, much of their wisdom has been lost through years of religious and cultural suppression. But in Bodhmall's teaching of her young nephew, we can perhaps see how they might have worked: by observing and learning from the natural world.

SADHBH

PRONUNCIATION: SYV
ALSO KNOWN AS: SADB, SIVE, DEER WOMAN

Sadhbh was a beautiful lady of the Otherworld whose tragic fate has inspired many retellings. Not much is known about her life before her central story, though she may have been a daughter of the Tuatha Dé Danann king Bodhbh Dearg, or be connected with the human king Conn of the Hundred Battles. As for the ending...well, fair warning: This is one of those Irish love stories that starts out tragic and ends worse.

THE STORY YOU NEED TO KNOW

Not much is known about Sadhbh's early life and childhood. She grew up in the Otherworld but was driven into the mortal realm with a curse put on her because she had rejected the advances of a terrible druid, Fer Doirich (which means "dark man"). In retaliation, Fer Doirich turned her into a deer and drove her into the mortal world. She survived alone for three years. A servant of the dark druid took pity on her and told her that if she managed to set foot in the fort of the Fianna, she would be restored to her human form. Sadhbh knew this would be difficult when the Fianna were known for their love of hunting deer.

Hunting one day, the leader of the Fianna, Fionn Mac Cumhaill, who presided over the warriors who lived off the land and roamed freely throughout the whole island of Ireland, observed strange behavior from his hounds (the entry on Uirne will explain that). They'd run out ahead of the rest of the Fianna in pursuit of a white deer, but Fionn's hounds

Bran and Sceolan weren't trying to bring the deer down. They seemed to be almost…playing with her. Having a certain insight into human-to-animal transformation, they had recognized Sadhbh the deer for who she truly was.

Fionn decided to hang back and let his hounds do their work, trusting their intuition. Soon, they turned homeward, and snarled to defend the deer from all the other hounds. With Fionn following, they led her safely into Fionn's home at Almhuin. There, she transformed, stunning the Fianna. Fionn, in particular, was taken with her sad story and promised to protect her.

Very soon, they fell deeply in love. Sadhbh did not venture outside of Fionn's home, afraid that the druid who cursed her would find her again. Fionn began to neglect his friends to spend his time with her.

Fionn was eventually called away to battle, and while he was away, Sadhbh realized she was with child. She then saw a man who looked just like Fionn trudging up the path toward Almhuin, with two hounds at his heels. Delighted to see her beloved, she ran to him. Too late—she saw it was Fer Doirich's magical disguise. His savage hounds lunged at her, and he struck her with his hazel wand, turned her back into a deer, and dragged her off to a hidden valley.

Fer Doirich kept Sadhbh in a narrow valley with no way in or out, visiting her from the Otherworld every day. In this captivity, she gave birth to a little boy, Oisín—Fionn's son. She was able to protect her son until the day came that Fer Doirich refused to leave without her, insisting that she come with him into the Otherworld and submit to his lust. Eventually, after pleading, coaxing, and berating her all day to no avail, he lost his temper and dragged her into the Otherworld, leaving the child behind.

Fionn never stopped looking for Sadhbh. Many years later, hunting once more, he thought he saw her in her deer form and killed his faithful hound Sceolan to protect her, but he could never be sure if it was her.

OISÍN

Pronunciation: UH-sheen (Ireland), OSH-an (Wales)
Also Known As: Osian, Ossian, Osheen, Deer Child

Oisín was the quintessential warrior poet. It was clear from the outset that Oisín, the son of Fionn Mac Cumhaill and Sadhbh, would be someone special. His name is the Irish word for a fawn or young deer, and his story is perhaps the most famous in all of Irish mythology.

The Story That You Need to Know

Oisín was discovered as a wild child on a hillside after his mother, Sadhbh, was dragged away to the Otherworld. Fionn managed to recognize him and took him in, but it was only years later that the boy was able to fill in his father on his early life, and on his deer-mother's sad fate.

Oisín became a great warrior of the Fianna but was also well known for his songs and poems. Oisín's skill in battle rivaled his father's, while his skill with words surpassed Fionn's. One day, while the Fianna were hunting in the woods near the modern-day Dublin suburb of Tallaght, a beautiful golden-haired woman astride a white horse appeared before them. She introduced herself as Niamh Cinn-Óir (meaning "Niamh of the Golden-Hair"), daughter of Manannán Mac Lir, and declared that she had fallen in love with Oisín of the Fianna from afar after hearing his beautiful poetry and tales of his great deeds. She asked him to run away with her and marry her in the Otherworld.

Oisín was all for it, but his father, Fionn, had his reservations. Fearing that he would never see his son again, Fionn placed a *geis* on Oisín: to return within three years. Oisín assured his father that he'd be home sooner than that, and leaped onto the back of the white horse.

The horse bore the pair across the sea to Tír na nÓg, a land ruled by Niamh's father (Manannán Mac Lir) and identified in some tales as the Isle of Man. The couple were welcomed with a year-long wedding feast, which gave way to a life of ease and plenty. There was no sickness, age, or death on Tír na nÓg, and there was always some amusement—a hunt, a feast, or a game—to distract Oisín from his growing homesickness.

Eventually, he could be put off no longer and asked Niamh for her white horse so that he could visit his father and all of his friends. Niamh reluctantly gave in after much argument, but she warned him that more time had passed than he realized, either because time moves differently in the Otherworld, or because he had simply not noticed the passage of time with no sickness or age to mark it. She warned him not to touch the soil of Ireland or he would never return.

Dismissing her warnings, Oisín set off. Returning to Ireland, he wondered if he'd taken a wrong turn. The great forests were gone, replaced by stone walls around small fields. The people were small, thin, and feeble. They gaped at him. He rode his white horse all over, calling out to ask for news of the Fianna and the great heroes he was familiar with. No one answered.

Eventually, he found the ruins of Fionn's great dun at Almhuin, and this convinced him that his wife had told the truth. He had been gone for hundreds of years, perhaps more. With his heart breaking in his chest, Oisín turned back to Tír na nÓg. On his way to the coast, he saw ten men struggling to move a boulder out of the way of a plow. Unthinkingly kind, as befitted a man of the Fianna, he bent down to pick up the stone. As he easily tossed it aside, the girth of the saddle snapped, and Oisín fell to earth.

The white horse sprang away and Oisín aged hundreds of years in an instant.

Some stories say that he died there and then, or even turned to dust. Other tales have it that he was brought to meet Saint Patrick, who was at the time considered the wisest man in Ireland. Oisín and Patrick (in some versions, they were joined by Caoilte) discussed stories, philosophy, and the new religion of Christianity. Whether Oisín converted to Christianity on his deathbed or died staunch in his pagan beliefs very much depends on the storyteller.

Some tales claim that the first place Oisín went to when he finally died was not to the part of the Otherworld where his wife lived, but to find his mother, Sadhbh, and that the two were reunited there at long last.

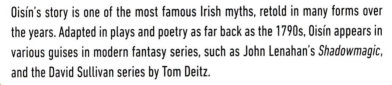

Now You Know

Oisín's story is one of the most famous Irish myths, retold in many forms over the years. Adapted in plays and poetry as far back as the 1790s, Oisín appears in various guises in modern fantasy series, such as John Lenahan's *Shadowmagic*, and the David Sullivan series by Tom Deitz.

DIARMUID

PRONUNCIATION: DEER-MID
ALSO KNOWN AS: DIARMUID UA DUIBHNE, DIARMUID OF THE LOVE SPOT

Diarmuid Ua Duibhne was famous for his skill as a warrior, wielding both a light spear for wounding known as the Yellow Spear (or Gáe Buide) and a heavy, killing spear (the Red Spear, or Gáe Dearg). He was most famous, however, for his "love spot" (or *Bol Sherca* in Irish), a magical mark on his forehead that made anyone who saw it fall in love with him. Diarmuid plays the romantic lead in many stories, often the one who wins the heart of a fair (and Otherworldly) maiden of mysterious origin. In adventures, he is often paired with the blunt and ugly Conán Maol as the two make for a comedic clash of personalities.

THE STORY YOU NEED TO KNOW

Diarmuid's name links him with a region of southwest Ireland in modern-day Kerry. When he was a child, his mother had two husbands, Roc and Donn, and Diarmuid, the son of Donn, grew up with his half-brother, the son of Roc. One day, as the children played, Donn was overcome with a fit of sudden jealousy and murdered Diarmuid's half-brother. In grief, Roc put a spell on the child's body, transforming it into a wild boar and sending it into the wilderness with a *geis* to hunt the son of Donn. Young Diarmuid received a complementary *geis*: never to pierce the skin of a boar, as his half-brother was now one.

After this tragic episode, young Diarmuid was fostered by Aengus Óg, growing up to become a beautiful and skilled warrior. He passed the tests to join the Fianna and took his place among a new, younger generation of heroes—a peer of Oisín with Fionn and older members as mentors and father figures.

Over the years, Diarmuid had a great many adventures with the Fianna. For example, he fell in love with a princess from the Land Under Wave, but had to sacrifice his love for her to save her life. He also saved Fionn Mac Cumhaill from a curse that stuck him to the ground while an army invaded, single-handedly fighting off the invaders at a ford and bringing back the sorcerer's blood to free Fionn and his companions. Through it all, he journeyed in and out of the Otherworld, learning strange lessons, seeing strange sights, and winning strange battles.

After many years, Diarmuid unwillingly ran away with Fionn's bride-to-be, Gráinne. She put a *geis* on him to run away with her, and he countered with a *geis* demanding that she come to him "neither naked nor clothed, neither indoors nor out, neither on foot nor on horseback." When Gráinne turned up in the doorway, dressed only in a blanket and astride a goat, he knew he'd met his match. Pursued relentlessly by the Fianna for running away with Fionn's fiancée, Diarmuid still found ways to stay connected with them, taking terrible risks just to get a glimpse of his old friends. He hid in a magical rowan tree and played *fidchell* (an ancient Irish form of chess) against Fionn by dropping berries on the board to show Oisín where to move his pieces. Fionn realized what was happening when Oisín won the match, as only Diarmuid had ever defeated him at the game.

After years on the run, Gráinne managed to negotiate a peace with Fionn, but Diarmuid was no longer counted as a member of the Fianna. Though he had his own family now, he missed his life of adventure terribly.

One day, Fionn came with an olive branch and asked Diarmuid to join the Fianna in a hunt. Diarmuid accepted without hesitation and didn't even back out when he found out that the Fianna were going after a terrible boar—the wild boar of Ben Bulben, which had been terrorizing the countryside. Remembering his childhood *geis*, Diarmuid only brought his light spear and hoped to stay out of the way.

On the hunt, the wild boar targeted Diarmuid alone, ignoring all the rest of the Fianna. At last, it charged and gored him. He managed to use the butt of his spear to crush the boar's skull, keeping the letter of his *geis* by not piercing its skin. There was still hope for his survival.

Mortally wounded, Diarmuid begged Fionn to magically heal him with a drink from his cupped hands. Fionn brought the water, but at the last moment, his old jealousy returned and he let the water trickle away before Diarmuid could drink. The same thing happened the second time, but the third time, Fionn had truly put his jealousy aside, and poured the water into Diarmuid's open mouth.

It was too late. Diarmuid lay dead, his transformed half-brother dead beside him.

Now You Know

Diarmuid is one of the great heartthrobs of Irish mythology. He was not just a pretty face, however—this warrior was fierce, and his love even stronger. The name "Diarmuid" is still common today, and W.B. Yeats's contemporary Lady Gregory wrote an early twentieth century play titled *Grania* that is based on the epic love story between Diarmuid and Gráinne.

GRÁINNE

PRONUNCIATION: GRAW-NYA

Raised as the daughter of one of the greatest High Kings of Ireland, Gráinne gave up her life of luxury and privilege in pursuit of true love. Passionate, headstrong, and clever, she is remembered as one of the great lovers of Irish myth.

THE STORY YOU NEED TO KNOW

As the youngest daughter of the great High King Cormac Mac Airt and Queen Eithne, Gráinne was raised with every advantage. As a noblewoman and king's daughter, it was important that she marry someone who was her equal. As Gráinne came of age, she knew her worth and rejected suitor after suitor for not living up to the same high standards she held herself to.

Secretly, Gráinne had fallen in love many years before. While watching a hurling match against a group of boys from the southwest, she only had eyes for one player. Nimble, lithe, and athletic, he wore his dark hair long over his forehead. When a gust of wind blew his hair off his forehead and she saw his face, young Gráinne was smitten. Over the years, she found a pretext to reject every suitor presented to her, assuming that the boy from the hurling field would turn up.

Eventually, she gave up the childish dream of a happily ever after. She resolved to accept the next suitable proposal she received. Soon after that, the messenger Dear Dubh arrived from none other than the captain of the great Fianna, Fionn Mac Cumhaill. Fionn was famously wise, handsome, and a master strategist, and even Gráinne couldn't say that he was not her equal. With no reason to refuse, she accepted.

At the wedding feast, Gráinne hid behind a curtain to catch her first glimpse of her husband-to-be. When she saw him, she was horrified. Fionn was an old man—far too old for her. His son, Oisín, was of a more appropriate age. Just as she was lamenting her choice, Fionn moved aside and she saw another of the captains of the Fianna. Her heart sank when she recognized the boy from the hurling field, who turned out to be Diarmuid. Using a sleeping potion on the host and after an exchange of *geasa*, Gráinne managed to persuade a reluctant Diarmuid to run away with her.

They were pursued relentlessly by the Fianna but were assisted by Aengus Óg. Sites referred to as the "beds of Diarmuid and Gráinne" litter the Irish landscape to this day—as they fled across the island, they slept in trees, at dolmens (stone monuments), and inside caves. Aengus Óg advised the couple to never eat where they cooked their food; never sleep where they ate; and never rise in the morning in the same place as they first bedded down—in other words, they should get up and move in the middle of the night.

At first, Gráinne's relationship with Diarmuid was chilly. She was irrevocably in love, but he saw her as the person who had forced him to betray Fionn and leave his friends. One day, as she crossed a stream with her skirts held up high, a drop of water splashed against Gráinne's thigh. She taunted Diarmuid that the water drop had more courage in it than he did. Things heated up between them after that, and Diarmuid grew to love her dearly. They had four children together while on the run.

After years of the great pursuit (or *toraíocht* in Irish) by the Fianna, Gráinne was party to many adventures. Diarmuid fought off giants, mercenaries, and his former friends, while Gráinne learned to live off the land and raise her children with lasting love and by trusting her wits.

She eventually managed to get in touch with her parents and have them mediate a settlement with Fionn and the Fianna. The lovers were allowed to settle into their own household, but Diarmuid was no longer welcome with the Fianna. To make peace between them, Gráinne hosted a year-long feast, during which old scores and wounds were settled.

After Diarmuid's tragic death, some stories say that Gráinne and Fionn found common ground in their grief, eventually getting married after all. Other stories tell of her daughter, the brilliant Eachtach, who decided to take revenge for her father's death, becoming the only warrior to defeat Fionn Mac Cumhaill in single combat.

Now You Know

Gráinne is one of the great lovers of Irish myth, and her story is woven throughout the Irish landscape. It was once a custom in the Irish countryside that if a man and a woman went to one of Diarmuid and Gráinne's "beds," the man could ask anything of the woman and she was not allowed to refuse! Their story has been retold many times in Irish literature, particularly in the 1901 play *Diarmuid and Grania* by W.B. Yeats and George Moore. More recently, a version of the story is recounted in the 2010 film *Leap Year*. The 2001 stage adaptation by Paul Mercier transposes the story to modern-day Dublin and was adapted into a 2015 film *The Pursuit*.

UIRNE

PRONUNCIATION: URR-na
ALSO KNOWN AS: TUIREN, TUIRREAN, TUIREANN

Aunt of the great warrior Fionn Mac Cumhaill, Uirne is mostly remembered for her great beauty and grace…and for her unusual children Bran and Sceolan, who were born as hounds. Bran and Sceolan nevertheless became famous members of the Fianna in their own right, proving that in some cases, pets really are family.

THE STORY YOU NEED TO KNOW

Uirne caused quite a stir among the men and women of the Fianna when she visited her sister Muirne's son Fionn. She was said to be as graceful as a river, and everyone hoped that she would flow in their direction. Fionn was quite happy to make sure that she made a good match and noticed that though she inspired poetry in the Fianna warrior Lugaid Lága, her mere presence was enough to render him mute with embarrassment.

Uirne's eye was caught by none of the Fianna, but by an Ulster king called Uileann (sometimes also called Illean Eachtach). Uileann married her with her famous nephew's blessing, on the condition that Fionn could send for her whenever he wanted, to ensure that Uileann was treating her right.

What Uileann didn't reveal was that he had a secret: a Sidhe (faery) lover called Uchtdealbh of the Fair Breast. Uchtdealbh missed her mortal lover Uileann, and when she found out that he had married another,

PART 4: Heroes & Villains   239

she was furious, and came up with a vindictive plot to get Uirne out of the way.

As far as Uileann and Uirne were concerned, married life was going very well indeed. One day, a messenger from Fionn arrived at the door, none other than Dear Dubh, Fionn's most trusted messenger, summoning Uirne to come and visit Fionn. They'd only been married a few months, but a promise is a promise, and so Uirne went with the messenger.

Much to her shock and bewilderment, once they got to a sufficiently out-of-the-way place, Dear Dubh transformed into a strange, angry Sidhe woman, who ranted and raved at Uirne for a while before turning her into a wolfhound! Poor Uirne had no idea what was going on and was even more bewildered when the Sidhe woman put back on her Dear Dubh disguise and dragged her on a leash to the house of King Fergus of Galway.

Fergus was renowned all across Ireland for his hatred of hounds, and Uirne-the-hound was terrified of him. Even she had heard stories of his cruelty, such as how he only employed servants who would throw sticks at dogs when he asked them to.

Even in this new form, Uirne's personality was still present. At first, she was so pitiful that even the cruel King Fergus was moved to put his hand on her head. And then she began to show her cleverness. When he took her hunting, she showed her fierceness and bravery. As time went on, her life as a woman began to fade away, and she became very contented with her life as a hound, especially with a king who doted on her. Soon the hound Uirne began to show signs of being ready to give birth– her human honeymoon had been long enough to get pregnant. And King Fergus was thrilled when she gave birth to two puppies—a small litter for a hound, but a large one if she'd still been human.

While Uirne was getting used to a dog's life, Uileann spent a long time thinking she was away visiting her nephew, while Fionn spent as long a time thinking she was content with her husband. Then one day, Fionn decided to call on his aunt. After some confusion, Uileann realized what must have happened. With Fionn's threats ringing in his ears, he rushed to his old meeting place with his faery lover and begged for her help.

Uchtdealbh was very smug about the trick she'd played. Uileann begged her to bring Uirne back, lest Fionn cut his head off. Uchtdealbh agreed, on condition that his head, and everything below it, would belong to her from that day on.

With Uchtdealbh's help, Uirne was restored to her humanity, with mostly pleasant memories of her life as a hound. She decided to get remarried to the tongue-tied Lugaid Lága, once she was absolutely certain he didn't have any magical ex-girlfriends kicking around.

King Fergus was sorry to lose his favorite hound but went on with his life with a new appreciation for a four-legged friend. And as for Uirne's pups, Bran and Sceolan? They could not be turned back into human form, because they had never lived as humans at all. So they remained hounds for all their lives.

Bran's coat was brindled, with many colors all blending into one. The other, Sceolan, was white with a red stripe down her spine. They both had the intelligence of humans but the loyal hearts of dogs. They became Fionn's best and favorite hunting hounds, accompanying him on countless adventures. After all, they were (literally) family!

Now You Know

Fionn Mac Cumhaill is often depicted with two wolfhounds by his side. There are a number of different stories of the origins of these wonderful hounds, and there's always something magical about them. Uirne seems to have lived happily after her adventure as a hound, because there are no more stories about her after this one.

CAOILTE

PRONUNCIATION: KWEEL-TCHA, KEEL-TA
ALSO KNOWN AS: CAÍLTE, CAELTE, KEELTA, KYLTA

Among the members of the Fianna, fleet-footed messengers were given high status. One thin gray man, Caoilte Mac Ronán, was the swiftest—able to run so fast that he could cross over into the Otherworld.

THE STORY YOU NEED TO KNOW

At one time, Fionn and the then–High King of Ireland were at odds. The High King felt that the Fianna were too strong of a force and had stirred up rebellion in the provinces, and he wanted a symbolic, and very public, dressing down. Fionn proposed that he come for a visit. It would be made public that he was the king's hostage, but in fact he'd stay for a civil visit; the two could feast and share stories, and after a suitable time had elapsed, Fionn would go free without repercussions. And the people of Ireland would see that the High King could constrain even the great Fionn Mac Cumhaill and be in no doubt as to who was in charge of whom.

The scheme was going off without a hitch, but there was one warrior who hadn't gotten the message: Caoilte Mac Ronán. He'd last been seen chasing a boar from the Otherworld, the two of them running so fast that they ran out to sea, over the waves, without slowing.

Before Fionn's false imprisonment was up, Caoilte returned. Finding out that Fionn was held hostage, he couldn't accept the dishonor done to his captain. Caoilte flew into a rage, going on a crazed rampage through the countryside. When he reached the king's home in Tara, there was no reasoning with him, but letting Fionn go early would undermine the whole exercise. So, the High King asked Caoilte to assemble two of every kind of bird and animal in Ireland.

This didn't buy as much time as he'd hoped, as Caoilte arrived that very evening, driving a tumultuous rabble of panicked animals before him. The High King stalled again, sending word to Caoilte that it was too dark to properly inspect the animals, and he'd have to wait until morning. Caoilte was directed to a house with seven windows and nine doors, all open, where he and the animals could spend the night. Caoilte spent an exhausting night running from window to door, stopping the animals from escaping. He got no sleep, and neither did anyone else, thanks to the cacophony of noise all the creatures made.

In the morning, the pre-arranged hostage release went off smoothly, and before anyone could invent the word "zoo," all the gathered animals bolted to the four corners of Ireland.

Some stories say that Caoilte's ability to run between worlds allowed him to live longer than the rest of the Fianna, eventually leading to his reunion with Oisín in his old age. This long lifespan was more of a curse than a blessing, though, and he finally deserted Ireland, heartbroken that all his friends were gone.

Now You Know

Caoilte appears in numerous tales of the Fianna as a peer of Fionn Mac Cumhaill. His ability to run across the water—and run between the mortal world and the Otherworld—conjures up images of modern superheroes, like the Flash.

FURTHER READING

We hope that this volume has whetted your appetite to discover more of the richness of Celtic mythology. For those who wish to dive in, we recommend these resources.

Books

A Dictionary of Celtic Mythology by James MacKillop; Oxford University Press. This is an invaluable reference guide with a wealth of well-researched information.

The Lore of Ireland: An Encyclopaedia of Myth, Legend and Romance by Dáithí O hOgáin; Boydell Press. Essential for anyone who wants to dig deeper into Irish myth.

Ireland's Immortals: A History of the Gods of Irish Myth by Mark Williams; Princeton University Press. A fantastic look at the gods of Irish myth that cuts through a lot of the fantastical reimaginings that passed for scholarship during the Celtic Revival.

The Arthur of the Welsh: The Arthurian Legend in Medieval Welsh Literature, edited by Rachel Bromwich, A.O.H. Jarman, and Brynley Roberts; University of Wales Press. A deep dive into the origins of Arthur in Welsh myth.

Old Ways, Old Secrets: Pagan Ireland by Jo Kerrigan; O'Brien Press Ltd. A blend of cultural custom, story, and place with modern relevance.

The Táin: From the Irish Epic Táin Bó Cuailnge, translated by Thomas Kinsella; Oxford University Press. The standard by which all other books about the *Táin* are judged. Illustrated with evocative ink work by Louis le Brocquy.

Finn and the Fianna by Daniel Allison; The History Press. A wonderful, modern collection of Fianna stories.

Legendary Ireland by Eithne Massey; The O'Brien Press. A great selection of tales linked to specific places in Ireland. Great for anyone planning a trip!

Táin: The Women's Stories by Karina Tynan; Connolly Books. Beautifully illustrated and poetic, evocative tales from the often-overlooked women of the *Táin*.

Listen to the Land Speak by Manchán Magan; Gill Books. A call to reconnect with the epic landscape.

ONLINE RESOURCES

There is a large collection of Celtic material free to read online at SacredTexts.com. While some of the scholarly texts are a little dubious in their methods and conclusions, there are also some fantastic resources there, including:

- *Gods and Fighting Men* by Lady Augusta Gregory
- *Cuchulain of Muirthemne* by Lady Augusta Gregory
- *The Mabinogion* translated by Lady Charlotte Guest
- *Four Ancient Books of Wales* by William F. Skene
- *The Poems of Ossian* translated by James Macpherson

These websites give an in-depth account of the Welsh mythological cycle:

www.mabinogi.net

www.mabinogion.info

A more academic collection of Irish manuscripts can be found at the digitized University College Cork archives at https://celt.ucc.ie/publishd.html.

The National Folklore Collection maintains an archive of Irish manuscripts and folklore at www.duchas.ie.

The National Library of Wales has an online exhibition of medieval Welsh manuscripts at https://library.wales/discover-learn/digital-exhibitions/manuscripts/the-middle-ages.

Podcasts

Story Archaeology by Chris Thompson and Isolde Carmody is a series of conversations between an academic and a storyteller, primarily focused on Irish mythology.

House of Legends: World Myths & Legends by Daniel Allison covers world mythology, with a focus on Scottish and Welsh mythology, interviewing many other storytellers.

The Candlelit Tales Podcast by the authors of this book is available on all podcasting platforms, where these stories and many more are retold to original music.

GLOSSARY

ANNWN:
The Welsh word for the Otherworld—that place of spirits and creatures and mystery that lies right alongside reality, separated by the thinnest veil.

AOS SÍ/AOS SIDHE:
Literally means "folk of the Sí/Sídh," or faery folk. See *Sidhe*.

BEALTAINE/BELTANE:
The Celtic Fire Festival near the beginning of May that ushered in the summer season. Concerned primarily with protection and conserving the household's luck for the coming season of scarcity.

CAIRN:
A human-made pile of stones. Sometimes, but not always, markers of a burial place. Sometimes placed on hilltops. There are many ancient cairns on the Celtic Archipelago, dating back to the Neolithic period.

CONTINENTAL CELT:
The Celts were not confined to the islands of the Celtic Archipelago. They originated on the continent of Europe and many Celtic tribes persisted there.

EMAIN MACHA:
The fort and the seat of the king of Ulster. This is also where the Boys-Troop was set up to train young warriors. It exists in Ireland today, more commonly called Navan Fort, and archaeological evidence points to it being a ritual site.

Fian/Fianna:

Young warriors would join a *fian*, a singular group to go out and rewild themselves. Under Fionn's leadership, all the seperate *fianna* were joined for the first time under the perfect mythic example of the Fianna.

Fomorian:

A supernatural race of people from under the sea, based out of Tory Island, the northernmost island off the coast of Ireland. They are often in opposition to the inhabitants of Ireland at any given time. Because of this, they are often vilified when later retellers want to set up an "evil" to set against the "good" land-dwellers.

Geis/Geasa:

A magical prohibition. Breaking a *geis* would bring doom from the Otherworld, and so observance of one's *geasa* was taken extremely seriously.

Imbolc/Imbolg:

The Celtic Fire Festival near the beginning of February that marks the start of spring. Celebrated in Ireland today as Brigid's Day. Crosses of reeds are woven for protection, and the festival is particularly associated with healing, rebirth, and artistic inspiration.

Mabinogi:

Translated as "moon stories" or "tales of a hero's boyhood," the *Mabinogi* is also referred to as the Mabinogion (though this is not grammatically correct in Welsh). The *Mabinogi* is a collection of four main "branches" of stories set in Wales. The character Pryderi is the only one to appear in all four branches, though he is not central to all of them. These stories mostly focus on the rulers of Wales and their adventures.

Newgrange/Brú na Bóinne:

One of the most famous neolithic sites in Ireland (it is older than the pyramids of Egypt). The passageway is aligned with the rising sun of the winter solstice in a remarkable feat of ancient architecture. Its exact significance is unknown as the tomb-builders died out. In mythology it is associated with Aengus Óg and the goddess Boann.

Otherworld:

A place that is both physical and metaphorical, that lies alongside reality and permeates the everyday while simultaneously existing under hills, under water, and on innumerable islands. The Otherworld is a central philosophical concept in Celtic myth. It is the realm of gods and magical creatures, separated from the real world by the thinnest of veils.

Samhain:

The main Celtic Fire Festival at the beginning of November, marking the beginning of winter and the Celtic New Year. Many of the traditions of Halloween that we celebrate today are drawn from Samhain. The veil between this world and the Otherworld is lifted, and the ancestors come through, along with ghosts, creatures, and magic from the Otherworld. Particularly potent for fortune-telling, many Irish customs center around looking toward the year ahead.

Sidhe/The Good People/The Other Crowd:

As the gods of the Celts came into conflict with Christianity, their status was changed. Belief in them did not cease, but it did shift. They became known as the people of the sidhe mounds (a term for the mysterious stone cairns and neolithic passage tombs that dot the landscape). It was believed that they lived in these mounds, and so they were called the Daoine Sidhe ("the people of the sidhe mounds") or Aos Sidhe ("folk of the sidhe mounds"), which was shortened to the Sidhe. Because the Otherworld was always immanent, it was considered sensible to speak of them in euphemistic terms lest they be eavesdropping and take offense.

SINGLE COMBAT:

In war, the Celts emphasized minimizing casualties as much as possible. There was no glory in slaughter. For this reason, there was an important rite called single combat, which was a one-on-one battle between single champions from each side. The war was decided based on who won the single combat. This was modified in *Táin Bó Cúailnge* to be a series of single combats between the lone Ulster defender and an entire invading army.

TÁIN:

The Irish word for cattle raid. There are many stories of *táins* in Irish myth, the most famous being *The Cattle Raid of Cooley* (a place in the northeast of Ireland). Extending far beyond a mere cattle-rustling expedition, it is a sweeping tale of divided loyalties, supernatural intrusions, betrayal, heartbreak, and destruction.

TÍR FO THUINN:

Literally "Land Under Wave." Sometimes the concept of the Otherworld in Celtic mythology is very diffuse, and in other stories it has a specific location. Tír fo Thuinn was that part of the Otherworld that existed deep under the sea, where there was dry land, running rivers, and castles of the Otherworldly people.

Tír na nÓg:

Literally "Land of Eternal Youth." This is one specific island among many others of the Celtic Otherworld that crops up in the story of Oisín. No one on this island gets sick, grows old, or knows any sadness, and it is always summer there. Sometimes geographically identified as the Isle of Man.

Tuatha Dé Danann:

The people of the goddess Danu. These became widely known as the Irish gods and goddesses. After Christianity, they were conflated with the faery folk.

Tylwyth Teg:

Similar to how the Daoine Sidhe of Irish myth went from being gods to being morally ambiguous creatures of the Otherworld, the Tylwyth Teg in Wales suffered the same fate. The belief in them changed, but did not diminish.

Wild Hunt:

Often the Sidhe, or faery folk, come from the Otherworld into the mortal realm to hunt. They are seen in a hunting group, on horseback with hounds by their sides in the wild. Encountering them can be perilous, especially at times of year like Bealtaine when they are known to be on the move. Even if they were after different prey, the impulsive faery folk might decide to hunt an unfortunate human or compel them to join the hunt as riders, with no guarantee of their safety.

INDEX

A
Ábhartach, 99–102
Aengus Óg, 60–65, 67, 168, 184, 186, 232, 236, 249
Ailill, 195–196, 200, 209–210
Aillén Mac Midgna, 218
Airmid, 71–72
Amergin, 20, 191
Annwn, 12–13, 29, 247. *See also* Otherworld
Aoife, 56, 176, 187–188, 190
Aos Sí/Aos Sidhe, 123, 126, 247, 250
Arawn, 45–48, 51, 124, 143–145, 147–149
Arianrhod, 23, 31–34, 79–80
Arthur, King, 24, 63, 119–122, 130, 141, 161–163, 165–169, 196

B
Badb, 49, 54
Balor of the Evil Eye, 12, 20, 74–77, 80–82
Banshees, 89–95, 182
Baobhan Sìth, 99–102
Bards, 12, 19
Battle of Bosworth, 141
Battle of Gabhra, 94, 220
Battle of Tailtiu, 20, 39
Battle of the Plain of the Pillars, 19
Battles of Moytura, 19–20, 32, 60, 67, 71
Bealtaine/Beltane, 15, 85, 217, 247, 251
Bean Nighes, 91–95, 107, 182
Black Dog, 123–124
Boann, 60, 63, 67–69, 71, 249
Bodach, 96–98
Bodhbh Dearg, 134–135, 225
Bodhmall, 218, 222–224
The Book of Aneirin, 22
The Book of Invasions, 15–16, 155
Book of Leinster, 16
Book of Taliesin, 44
Book of the Dun Cow, 16
Boys-Troop, 178, 180–181, 205, 208, 247
Bran, King, 23–24, 35, 38, 52, 70, 142, 146–148, 151–156
Branwen, 23–24, 35, 52, 70, 146–148, 151–156
Brehon Law, 11–12, 165–166
Bres, King, 19, 60, 71–72, 76–77
Brown Bull of Cooley, 49, 133–135, 201, 209
Brownie, 88–90
Brú na Bóinne, 61–64, 67, 249

C
Caer, 65
Cai, Sir, 24, 120, 162, 166
Cailleach, 29, 41–44, 96–97
Cairns, 42, 202, 247, 249
Caitlín of the Crooked Teeth, 75–76, 80
Caoilte, 130–131, 220, 231, 242–243
Cath Dédenach Magh Tuireadh, 19–20
Cath Magh Tuiread, 18–19
Cath Palug, 24, 119–122, 162
Cathbad, 171, 180, 182, 184, 189, 205–206
Cathain, 100
The Cattle Raid of Cooley, 16, 133–135, 181, 190, 201–210, 250
Celtic calendar, 15
Celtic culture, 6–13, 22–28, 73, 83–87, 127–129
Celtic mythology
  ancient manuscripts, 15–24
  creation myth and, 14, 16
  creatures/monsters of, 7, 12–28, 42–48, 83–148, 157–159, 198, 220
  explanation of, 6, 8–28
  gods/goddesses of, 7, 10–27, 29–87, 100, 180, 202–205, 249–251

heroes/villains of, 7, 12, 21–25, 35–38, 48, 56, 64, 74, 77, 93–95, 100, 130, 142–243
revival of, 27–28
sources of, 14–25
Celts
communities of, 9–11, 13, 16
description of, 9–13
origin of name, 9
tribes of, 9–11, 21, 32, 49, 79, 137, 177, 247
Ceridwen, 41–44
Cesair, 16, 17
Cet, 191, 193, 195, 206
Cét-Cath Magh Tuireadh, 19
Christianity, 22–26, 33, 67, 77, 84, 87, 97, 109, 165, 171, 197, 231
Cian, 71, 76, 81
Colonialism, 20, 26–27
Conaire Mór, 21
Conall Cearnach, 44, 181, 189, 191–196, 206
Conchobar Mac Nessa, 49, 170–172, 184, 193–200, 203–210, 214–215
Connla, 176, 180, 187–190
Continental Celts, 9–10, 49, 79, 247
Cormac Mac Airt, 21, 37–38, 165–166, 235
Creatures/monsters, 7, 12–28, 42–48, 83–148, 157–159, 198, 220. *See also specific creatures/ monsters*
Cú Roi Mac Dáire, 182, 194–195

Cù-Sìth, 123–126
Cúchulainn, 21, 25, 38, 56, 93–94, 125, 173, 176–183, 186–196, 201, 206–210
Culann, 125, 178–180
Culhwch, 45, 62–63, 161–164, 166, 168
Cumhall, 217–218, 222–223
Cŵn Annwn, 123–125
Cygfa, 52, 148–149, 156–158
Cyhyraeths, 91–95, 182

D
Daghda, 19, 56, 59–61, 63–65, 68, 70
Danu, 31–34, 100, 251
Daoine Sidhe, 84–86, 250, 251
Deichtre, 44, 178, 184–186
Deimne, 217–218, 223–224
Deirdre, 204–205, 208, 211–216
Dian Cecht, 19, 56–57, 70–73
Diarmuid, 62, 64, 232–234, 236–237
Dindshenchas (*Lore of Places*), 16
Donn Cúailnge, 133–136, 200
Druids, 10, 12–13, 25
Dullahan, 93, 107–110

E
Each Uisce, 111–114
Efnisien, 35, 151–155
Eithlinn, 75–76, 80–81
Emain Macha, 171, 178, 188, 205, 208, 211, 247
Ewan MacLaine, 93, 107, 110

F
Faoladh, 127–131
Fear Dearg, 103–104
Fer Doirich, 225, 227
Ferdiad, 180–181
Fergus Mac Róich, 172, 201, 205–210, 214–215, 240–241
Fian/Fianna, 11, 16, 21, 62–64, 94, 97, 130, 134, 217–239, 242–243, 248
Fianna Cycle, 16, 21, 222
Findchoem, 191, 193
Finnbennach, 133–136, 200
Finnegas, 218
Fintan, 17, 19
Fionn Mac Cumhaill, 21, 26, 68, 142, 217–222, 225–228, 233–243
Fir Bolg, 18–19, 60, 71, 155
First Battle of Moytura, 19, 60, 67, 71
"First Branch of the Mabinogi," 22–23, 143
Fomorians, 17–19, 59–60, 71, 74–77, 80–81, 248
Fosterage, 10–11
Four Branches of the Mabinogi, 21–24, 47, 137, 143, 147, 150, 156, 248
Four cycles, 16–21, 24, 37–38
"Fourth Branch of the Mabinogi," 23, 47
Fuamnach, 63–64

G
Geis/geasa, 13, 21, 142, 187–189, 228, 232–236, 248
Gender, 10–11, 61

Index 253

Glossary, 247–251
The Gododdin, 22
Gods/goddesses, 7, 10–27, 29–87, 100, 180, 202–205, 249–251. *See also specific gods/goddesses*
Goll Mac Morna, 217–218, 220
Good People, 84–87, 249–250
Gráinne, 62, 64, 220, 233–238
Gwair ap Geirioedd, 24
Gwawl ap Clud, 51–53, 145, 158
Gwern, 153–154
Gwrgi Garwlwyd, 127–131
Gwrhyr Gwalstawt Ieithoedd, 163, 166
Gwri of the Golden Hair, 147–148
Gwydion, 23, 32, 79–80, 149
Gwyn ap Nudd, 45, 168
Gwyon Bach, 43–44

H
Hafgan, 45–47, 145
Headless horsemen/-women, 93, 107–110
Heroes/villains, 7, 12, 21–25, 35–38, 48, 56, 64, 74, 77, 93–95, 100, 130, 142–243. *See also specific heroes/villains*
High Kings, 21, 37–38, 43, 151, 197, 204, 220, 235, 242–243

I
Imbolc/Imbolg, 15, 33, 42, 248

J
Judges, 10, 12

K
Kelpies, 111–114
Kingdoms, 11, 21–23, 47, 51–52, 74, 129–131, 146–149, 154
Kings Cycle, 16, 21
Kingship, 11, 16–21

L
Languages, 9–11, 20–22, 26–27
Leabharcham, 211, 213–214
Lebor Gabála Érenn (*The Book of Invasions*), 15–16, 155
Lebor na hUidre (Book of the Dun Cow), 16
Leprechauns, 6, 82
Liath Luachra, 218, 222–224
Lleu Llaw Gyffes, 79–82
Llŷr, 24, 35–39, 52, 151, 159, 168
Lóegaire, 194–195
Lore of Places, 16
Lugaid Lága, 239, 241
Lugaid Mac Con Roi, 182
Lugh Lamhfada, 15, 20, 29, 60, 71, 77, 79–82, 181, 185–186, 211

M
Mabinogi, 21–24, 47, 137, 143, 147, 150, 156, 248
Mabon ap Modron, 24, 62–65, 168
Mac Cecht, King, 20, 57
Mac Cuill, King, 20, 57
Mac Gréine, King, 20, 57
Macha, 49–54, 181, 204

Magicians, 12, 15
Manannán Mac Lir, 20, 35–39, 81, 94, 97, 156, 214, 228, 230
Manawydan, 23–24, 35, 52–53, 148–151, 154, 156–159, 168
Math fab Mathonwy, 23, 32, 79–80, 149
Matholwch, 151, 153–154
Maura, 97–98
Mechi, 56–57
Medb, Queen, 26, 49, 65, 94, 142, 181, 194–202, 204–210
Merlin, 24, 44, 141
Merrows, 115–118
Miach, 71–72
Midir, 63–64
Morality, 12, 59, 155
Morrígan, 7, 42, 49, 54–57, 60, 71, 94, 100, 130, 173, 180, 182
Morrígu, 49, 54
Muirne, 218, 222–223, 239
Myrddin Emrys, 24, 140–141
Mythological Cycle, 16–21, 37–38
Mythology sources, 14–25

N
Naoise, 208, 213–215
Nemed, 18–19
Nessa, 170–172, 208
Newgrange, 61–64, 67, 249
Niall of the Nine Hostages, 21, 43
Niamh Cinn-Óir, 37, 228, 230
Nuada, King, 19, 60, 63, 67–68, 71–72, 82

O

Ochall Ochne, 134–135
Oisín, 37, 93–94, 220, 227–231, 233, 236, 243, 251
Olwen, 45, 62–63, 161–164, 166, 168
Other Crowd, 84–87, 249–250
Otherworld, explanation of, 7, 12–15, 25, 29, 249, 250

P

Paganism, 14, 24, 32, 53, 77, 87, 97, 109, 129, 165, 231
Partholon, 17–18
Priests, 12, 25
Pryderi, 23, 47–48, 52–53, 119, 145–150, 154, 156–158, 248
Púca, 88–90
Pwyll, 22–23, 47–53, 143–148, 154

R

Red Book of Hergest, 22
Red Dragon, 137–141
Redcap, 103–106, 115
Resources, 244–246
Rhiannon, 22–23, 49–53, 145–148, 156–158, 181, 204

S

Sadhbh, 225–228, 231
Saint Brigid, 15, 29, 32–33, 56, 248
Saint Patrick, 231
Samhain, 15, 42, 63, 85, 104, 130, 217–218, 249
Scathach, 25, 56, 173–177, 180–181, 187–188
Second Battle of Moytura, 19–20, 32, 60
"Second Branch of the Mabinogi," 23
Selkies, 81, 115–118
Sidhe, 63–64, 84–87, 93–94, 239–240, 247, 249–250
Single combat, 149, 175, 181, 201, 210, 237, 250
Sith, 84–86, 99, 102
Slua Sidhe, 85
Sons of Mil, 16, 20, 39, 94
Sons of Tuireann, 37, 211, 225
Sons of Uisneach, 205–209, 213–215
Storytelling, 8, 12–14, 19, 26
Súaltam Mac Róich, 184–186
Swineherds, 24, 119–120, 133–134

T

Táin Bó Cúailnge (*The Cattle Raid of Cooley*), 16, 133–135, 181, 190, 201–210, 250
"Third Branch of the Mabinogi," 23, 156
Tír fo Thuinn, 74–75, 250
Tír na nÓg, 230, 251
Tuatha Dé Danann, 14, 18–20, 31–32, 37–39, 54–63, 67–71, 76–82, 133–136, 185, 225, 251
Tylwyth Teg, 45, 84–86, 251

U

Uchtdealbh, 239–241
Uileann, 239–241
Uirne, 239–241
Ulster Cycle, 16, 21, 54, 133–134, 170, 184, 197, 203, 211

W

Werewolves, 127–131
White Book of Rhydderch, 22
White Dragon, 138–141
Wild Hunt, 45, 123, 168, 251
Wolfhounds, 123–130, 240–241
Wulvers, 127–131

Y

Y Ddraig Goch, 137–141
Ysbaddaden, 161–162

Take a mythical journey.

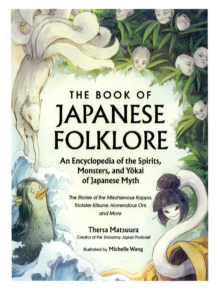
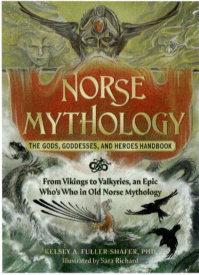

Pick up or download your copies today!